Don't Look Before You Leap...

You Leap...

by David Webb

Don't Look Before You Leap

by David Webb

Cover Art and Illustrations by Magdolna Gondon

Editing by Alison at FirstEditing.com

Written for my children Rachel, Robyn, Katie, David and Amy, so they will know a little more about their family, their dad and themselves.

I would like to thank my dad and my mom (Dick and Audrey Webb), and brothers, Andy and Brian, for living lives that provided me with so much good writing material. Thanks for being good sports about what I wrote, too. Thanks, Mom for taking such an interest in my writings. Without your laughter and insight, I never would have made it this far. To my loving wife, Eszter, who encouraged and assisted me in putting it all together.

CONTENTS

Lying Around

As luck would have it, both of my siblings turned out to be boys. One older. One younger. I was mercilessly sandwiched in the middle. Eking out an existence each day, barely surviving, I pressed forward against their treachery. My brothers might have a different take on the situation, but they are not writing this story.

Don't get me wrong, I love my brothers and have long since forgiven them for all their transgressions against me. However, I consider myself deprived in having only brothers and no sisters. Certainly my mother wanted a little girl and, now that I myself have three, I can truly understand why she did. Anyone can plainly see when compared to little boys, little girls bear a far closer resemblance to actual human beings, but my reasons for wanting a sister had nothing to do with any of that.

Sean, a friend of mine, once told me that he had regularly dated his sister's friends throughout adolescence. He even met his wife because she was his sister's roommate in college. What a racket! Every guy should be as fortunate. Well, I wasn't so blessed as to have a "Love Connection" hostess built right into my family unit. Girls were to remain a mystery to me longer than they did to most guys. I didn't figure them out until...., well, never mind, I guess I'll always remain a step behind in that regard.

Perhaps my predicament explains why, in the very distant past, I used to persecute my younger brother, Brian. In fact, that has to be the reason. There isn't any other logical explanation. Deep in the recesses of my mind I knew, instinctively, how advantageous it would be to have a younger sister, but what did I have? A crummy little brother. No wonder I felt awkward around girls. No wonder I couldn't get any dates. It had to be my little brother Brian's fault! The way I see it is that my brain, all on its own, concluded subconsciously, that Brian was the source of most of my problems. It was only justice that he suffer accordingly. Fortunately, today it is universally accepted that "society" is the root cause of all of our faults; therefore, I shouldn't be held responsible for the atrocities I heaped upon Brian.

Years ago, however, my antiquated parental units saw it differently. I was punished for the slightest infractions, like knocking out one of Brian's permanent front teeth, cutting his forehead open with a perfectly thrown tennis ball can, and making him smell my sweaty, stinky feet. The latter probably explains some of his strange behavior today. Even if he didn't suffer permanent brain damage from the ordeal, his olfactory nerve was probably rendered completely useless.

Truthfully, I can't remember being actually punished for any of the physical damage I caused to Brian. In fact, as

I recall, despite my constant harassment of Brian, I was rarely reprimanded for any of it. My parents didn't relish punishing us, but sometimes I committed infractions that they felt required their immediate attention. I suppose their goal was to ensure that I would never do whatever I was doing ever again. What were those violations? Unfortunately, I can't remember many of the specifics, with one exception — the Big Lie.

I knew after I was caught in the Big Lie, I was really in for it. Dread filled the air as I awaited the punishment that was coming to me when my father returned home from work. Since my mother didn't punish me on the spot, it was a sure sign that I had stepped far over the line this time. Delaying punishment was not her style. My parents employed completely opposite methods when it came to punishment. Why were their styles so different? Did they evolve in different directions while Dad was away in Vietnam, sort of how the strange creatures of Australia, separated from the other continents, took a different route in their development than the animals in the rest of the world?

If my parents' disciplinary styles were animals, Dad would definitely be the "elephant." When tasked to deal out the corrective action, my father was stoic and dignified. He never showed any anger no matter how horrible the infraction. He was just doing what had to be done to motivate us from the wrong path to the right one. I, for one, became very motivated to find that right path just before receiving what was coming to me. Like the elephant, Dad also had size. None of us would ever be as large as Dad who was 6 foot tall and as heavy as 220 pounds.

Dad's target was always the soft, padded buttocks. Just a few swats and it would be over. "You shouldn't choke your brother, blah, blah, blah...," he might say. Who listens to a lecture at a time like that? Just get it over with! I couldn't process too much information pre-spanking.

That pretty much sums up the downside of having Dad dole out the punishment. On the upside, with his technique, you knew exactly what you were up against. The same could not be said of my mother's technique. Actually, referring to my mom's method of punishment as a technique sort of makes it sound sophisticated. Sophistication had nothing to do with it. You may as well refer to a pig's technique of eating.

Mom's disciplinary style could best be labeled the "duck-billed platypus." There wasn't any rhyme or reason to it, which was understandable. Trapped in a home with three boys only a few years apart in age would have been enough to drive any mom insane. For my mom it was even worse because she couldn't rely on any help from my dad during both of his yearlong deployments to Vietnam.

Mom may have been patient, but when we finally pushed her over the edge – look out! She would take hold of the nearest object that remotely suited her needs in the same manner as a guy, focused on his weekend do-it-yourself project, grabs the closest available tool to use as a hammer. People who say women aren't as mechanical as men have never seen my mom wield a spatula, wooden spoon or ruler. The problem for mom was that she had no talent for racquet sports. If she had been a little more proficient at tennis, badminton or, at least, ping-pong, she might have been a threat. As it was, Mom rarely made contact with the skinny, toothpick-sized legs my brothers and I were sporting at the time, especially when we were jumping around the room.

Who had the more effective style, Mom or Dad? For overall effect, I'd have to give the nod to Dad; the psychological factor tipping the balance. Mom's forays were too spontaneous and unpredictable. For us, the anticipation of what was coming was worse than the punishment itself. Dad had Mom beat hands down in the anticipation department.

This dread of anticipation was to reach a new and higher plateau the day of the Big Lie. That day, in the spring of 1973 in Northern Virginia, started in a very ordinary fashion, probably differing little from the start of similar days for the Titanic, the Hindenburg, or almost any Amtrak departure. I was in the sixth grade. A friend of mine, Art, was coming over for a visit. Brian was in the basement doing what he did best – watching TV. My older brother, Andy, was most likely outside catching a frog, snake, or some similar creature. Dad was at the Pentagon and due to return at his usual time of six p.m. As Mom was heading out of the house to go shopping, she turned to me and doled out the usual dreaded task of practicing the piano.

I'd been taking piano since kindergarten, but you wouldn't know it. By the sixth grade I displayed about as much talent on the piano as a trained parrot, and that's assuming the parrot only uses its beak. Throw in the feet and the parrot had me beat, no contest. It's a long shot, but maybe if I had actually practiced a few times, I would have shown a little more proficiency. I wasn't much for practicing in the traditional sense of the word. To me, just being *assigned* a practice session was close enough to the real thing. It's sort of like putting vegetables on your plate, which if consumed, would be very healthy for you. Only, you don't actually eat the vegetables. Their mere presence should suffice as proof of your intention to be healthy. Why go to the effort of actually placing the unsavory objects into your mouth? Any kid knows that it's much wiser to save valuable stomach space for something more useful, like dessert.

In my life, piano practice and vegetables occupied a similar place of importance. I deduced the situation to be the following:

1. Mom tells me to practice the piano.
2. I don't actually get within ten feet of the piano, but I do glance at it from a safe distance.

3. I do something more enriching, like watching "Get Smart" reruns.
4. Later, Mom queries me, "Did you practice your piano today?"
5. I answer, "Yes."
6. She accepts my answer.
7. Mom's happy.
8. I'm happy.
9. The world is a better place.

Naturally, I'd never develop into the concert pianist my mom always wanted, but then again, how many concert pianists know what "Nitrowhisper'n" is? ("Get Smart" episode number 82).

Our "system" worked wonderfully for months. In fact, I became so accustomed to the system; I rarely considered practicing the piano at all. My mom accepted my word as though I were the Pope. We had a pretty nice and tidy arrangement going. Then, she had to go and screw it all up.

After Mom left the house with assurances from me that the day's practice would be accomplished, I settled down in front of the TV in the basement with Art and Brian for a little intellectual stimulation. After the show was over (and let me say it touched me deeply. I am a better person today because of that show, whatever it was), Art had to go home. As Art was walking out the door, my mother returned from her errands.

Her suspicion raised, she immediately inquired as to whether I had practiced the piano. I gave the rote, infallible answer, "Yes." Unbelievably, she asked me again. Still unperturbed, I responded again that I had. Then, she asked, "When?" *While she was gone of course!* I started to become greatly irritated and slightly nervous. Nothing like this interrogation had ever happened before. The Emperor had spoken, who was this vile creature that dared to question my word? But here she was, my mom becoming a regular super sleuth, like that lady in "Murder, She Wrote."

I hadn't committed murder, but you wouldn't know it the way Mrs. Sherlock Holmes went about piecing together evidence, mostly from my own testimony. Isn't there something in the Constitution against that? Unquestionably, there is, but as a hapless victim living in a tyrannical dictatorship, political documents were about as useful to me as sandpaper in a bathroom.

As Doom's dark cloud began to surround me, tightening its grip, desperation set in. Telling lie after lie, I went further down into the Abyss. I was in so deep; I concluded that descending a little, or even a lot, further into the Black Void of Lies wouldn't matter. I turned to the only surefire way of escape – an eyewitness.

Certainly, if I could produce an eyewitness to confirm the fact that I had practiced the piano, I could refute the prodigious amount of mere circumstantial evidence my mother was amassing. The small, but disturbing, fact that I had never actually practiced the piano was irrelevant. Like the Grinch, when he couldn't find a reindeer, I made my witness, instead. My unwitting conspirator would be nine year-old Brian. He just didn't know it – yet.

As I made a beeline for his locale in the basement, I congratulated myself on the brilliance of my plan. For in presenting Brian as my alibi, I would also eliminate the possibility that he could be asked by my maternal Agatha Christie if he had heard me playing the piano during her absence. In fact, I couldn't believe Mom had failed to see my brother as the obvious instrument of my undoing. "Too late for her," I thought as I whizzed down the stairs.

I minced no words with Brian. I let him know that the situation was critical. The only way to snatch me from the Jaws of Death was to march upstairs, go straight to Mom and tell her, "I heard David practice the piano today."

My wild eyes told him there would be no discussing or debating my orders.

Dragging him to the stairs, I sent him straightaway to my mom. After my veracious, irreproachable witness delivered his deposition, I would be able to stand unshaken before my accuser. I listened intently as Brian spoke:

"I….(wavering)…think….(fidgeting) …..he……might…..have…. practiced….(still greater wavering and fidgeting)….the………piano?"

Doomed! That was it! My star witness plan had backfired. How could this have happened? What is worse than believing you've nearly escaped, only to slip back into the grasp of your pursuer?

Now, with nothing to do but fearlessly face the executioner, I turned to mine with knees knocking and teeth clattering. My "Spider Sense" was going off of the scale this time. Danger was near and there was no escape. This was the whopper. I had bet everything, including the tender epidermis of my posterior, on number 7 and the wheel stopped on 13.

Time stood still. My mind was awash. I was in a trance. When I finally drifted back to the physical world, I found myself standing at attention in the middle of the kitchen with Brian next to me. Yes, Brian. Brutus! Judas! Benedict Arnold! It was all HIS fault. If only HE were a better liar, I wouldn't be in this mess.

There was no time to worry about a fitting punishment for him. Deep within myself, I was contemplating my own castigation. I shivered at the thought of what would happen when my father returned from the Pentagon. I hadn't received a single swat from Mom. That was not good. She was waiting for Dad. Eons passed. Finally, the silence was broken by the purr of an engine as my father's car pulled into the carport.

He stepped into the kitchen. The true culprit, Brian, would receive less than half the number of swats that were coming to me. Oh, the Humanity! Life is always cruelest to those who live close to the edge. Dad explained that "causing Brian to lie" was even worse than my own lies. Now I was being held responsible for Brian's lack of Academy Awarding winning acting skills! The question was not whether an Oscar was in Brian's future, but whether he had a future at all. My own future wasn't looking very promising either.

This time, I would need each and every fat cell on my backside to do its duty. I've always been self-conscious about having a rather round derriere. It's possible my distinguishing feature developed as a result of natural body defense mechanisms – a reaction to protect an exposed, vulnerable and frequently assaulted rump. I like to believe that I commanded myself in a dignified manner throughout the entire ordeal. That is, I didn't jump around the room like a jackrabbit and add additional, painful swats to my total.

It all ended quickly. Thinking I had survived the totality of my punishment, my spirits were up. However, when I returned downstairs, my mother announced that, in order to satisfy the full measure of my punishment, there was an additional task for me to perform. "Starting each day, as soon as you return from school," she declared, "you will pull every weed in our yard." I gasped at the unfairness of it all. It's one thing to be punished for punishment's sake, but this was slave labor. I thought slavery had been outlawed over one hundred years ago, but here, in the sanctuary of my own home, the vile practice was resurrected. Worst of all, I was the slave! I have always thought it a bit unrighteous to benefit from another's misfortune. Now, my own mother was using me as her personal gardener under the pretense that I was being rightfully punished.

From that day forward, I would view my confinement in school from a different perch. School was no longer a prison where my brain would fight to repel intrusions by math, English and social studies. Laurel Ridge Elementary became Nirvana; a sanctuary from the heat, the sweat, and the boredom of pulling stubborn, prickly weeds. The punishment wouldn't have been half bad except that I had the temerity to believe I could actually finish the job. How many tasks did Hercules have to perform? Twelve? Let me tell you, if one of his tasks was to pull every weed in our yard, he would have quit right there on the spot. I don't want to degrade the efforts of my parents to create a beautiful lawn, but after years of fertilizer, weekend gardening forays, and about a dump truck load of Weed-B-Gone, they achieved an enviable lawn of about ten percent grass and ninety percent weeds. As I scanned the lawn after days of laboring, it became obvious that the weeds were spreading faster than I could pull them up.

Thankfully, my father was reassigned to Ft. Huachuca, Arizona. His new assignment cut my punishment from a triple-life sentence to three weeks at hard labor. Did I learn my lesson? It would be disingenuous to say I have remained completely honest since that day I was caught, but thereafter, I have striven to be more truthful.

Proving that humans are able to overcome the negative psychological conditioning that occurred during their youth, I took up playing the piano again in my thirties. Some days I've been known to practice for hours. Since I still display less talent than a trained parrot and play the same songs over and over, I might be accused of seeking revenge against family members for the events of years ago. Nothing could be further from the truth. I truly enjoy playing the piano, even if *some* family members wish that I would just promise to practice, but not actually do it.

I vs Eye

Kevin, a friend of mine, frequently tells me, "You've won life's lottery." He certainly isn't referring to the real thing, because I would never buy an actual lottery ticket, even if the jackpot were two trillion dollars. To me, a jackpot of two trillion dollars only means that my odds of winning would be worse than if the jackpot were merely one trillion dollars. It's a philosophical thing. What I am saying is, if I thought I could actually win the lottery with odds against me many times greater than that of:

A. Crashing in an airplane
B. Being hit by a meteor or
C. Eaten by sharks in a hot tub

logically, I would never leave my house. Of course, that would result in my having a fabulous chance, by lotto standards, of dying by asphyxiation, or worse, when the house burned down.

What Kevin is referring to is my job. He thinks that as a pilot for a major airline, all that's left for me to do in this life is to...well...there's really nothing left for me to do. He says that I've "got it made," and that option "A," above, isn't going to happen. No credit is given for the fact that option "A" won't occur, because as the pilot, *I'm* going to make certain it doesn't happen.

My father, a 30-year Army colonel, felt the same way as Kevin. He incessantly joked, even while I was flying in the Air Force, as to when I was going to "start working" or "get a job." His jabs picked up intensity after I made the transition to the airlines. Justice was served when an issue of Money magazine came out the very month I was hired. Money had an article on the top 100 jobs in America. Yes, airline pilot was on the list—just a few spaces *behind* Army officer. Ha! "Long work hours" and "jet lag" were said to detract from a pilot's job. I guess I didn't realize how tough I was going to have it. However, it would have been nice if Money had included a warning about the nasty cases of sunburn an extended layover in the Caribbean can cause. That fact would knock airline pilot down another notch or two for sure.

Words cannot describe the emotion I felt as I held the phone to my ear awaiting the verdict from the Goddess of Fate in the airline's personnel department—hired or "How are you at panhandling?" When she told me that I was in, I hope she was holding the phone away from her ear, or she might be deaf today.

Getting this job was the completion of a doubtful journey that, at times, I didn't even know I was taking. To an outside observer, it might appear that I had planned this career path all along. After all, I left for the U.S. Air Force Academy at age 17, and began flying at 18. From there, I proceeded to USAF pilot training and elected to go to the "heavy" KC-10. At this point, many of my comrades waved an accusatory finger at me saying, "You're planning to go to the airlines, aren't you?!" This label was put on anyone who could have gone the fighter route, but chose instead to fly aircraft that looked more like a barge than a supersonic machine of death. I suppose I can see why those guys might think I was leaning a bit toward the commercial side. Next time I'm at work, I'll have to ask some of my fellow pilots to clarify those remarks.

No, while I was a kid, a cadet or attending pilot training, I never considered the airlines. Growing up, I was around some guys who, if they were kids today, would be major computer geeks. However, these guys didn't even own a computer, because back then, computers were larger than Bill Gates' auxiliary residence #4, which makes the White House look like a double-wide at a rundown trailer park. Instead, as an alternate way to show their geekability, every once in a while, as an airplane passed so far overhead that you could only make out the long white streak of its contrail, one of the guys would exclaim, "That's a Boeing 747," or "There goes a DC-10." I'd look at the contrail and do a "who cares" shrug of the shoulders. I knew nothing about airplanes, and didn't plan to learn anything about them. It is a bit ironic that I'm employed as a pilot today, while many of those guys have only gotten as close to a cockpit as Microsoft Flight Simulator will allow them.

Lack of foresight wasn't the only obstacle that I faced in the trek to my profession. As I began to consider a piloting career with the Air Force, I saw an assortment of barriers in my path. One question every pilot has to ask himself is: Do I have the ability, or the "Right Stuff" to be a pilot? The Right Stuff is that intangible knack for being able to fly and land an airplane in all conditions and situations. As Air Force pilots in training, we thought of the right stuff as flying the T-38 in three-foot "fingertip" formation while performing aerobatics (loops and rolls), or landing while in formation. Another problem was airsickness. Just how challenging is it to concentrate on your flight instruments while heaving into a barf bag? Not as challenging as trying to read those instruments through the goo when you miss the bag. The Right Stuff aside, the most difficult problem for me was getting to pilot training in the first place.

Two of the greatest obstacles I faced to stepping into a flight suit were my own parents. That's right—my parents, in that I didn't pick the right ones. Don't misread me here. My parents have always been of great encouragement to me, and except for the occasional walloping with the nearest available kitchen utensil, they are the finest a boy could have ever hoped for. The problem lies in their eyes. They can't see, at least not well enough to be pilots. I don't want to imply that they are blind, but Mom and Dad used to go around the house emitting high pitched squeaking noises to avoid colliding with the walls.

Squeaking is a fine method for finding one's way around the home, but it doesn't work very well in an airplane cockpit. Not that this mattered much to my mom, because she would just as soon take up cobra kissing as flying a supersonic airplane. My beef with my parents is that they had the nerve to pass on many of their visual maladies to me. This inheritance doomed me to spend much of my four years at the Academy and most of my meager wages trying to fight genetic injustice.

I found out, late in high school, that my eyes weren't quite up to snuff. This discovery was directly responsible for my voluntary incarceration at the federal penitentiary in Colorado—the USAF Academy, because only the Academy had a special waiver that allowed its new lieutenants with less-than-perfect 20/20 vision to attend pilot training. Knowing I was fated by my genes to wear goggles for the greater portion of my life, I plea bargained a four-year sentence and left for Colorado to seek excitement, adventure, and celibacy.

Soon after my arrival, I realized that I faced a great conundrum. My number one priority was to preserve my eyes; in other words, I didn't want to use them for any activities other than sleeping. However, the Academy had different goals for my life—a life that they now owned.

It wasn't so much the academic load. Any motivated person could complete each day's task in just under 39 ½ hours. The problem was that none of the textbooks were in Braille. It was becoming obvious that the Academy was going to require me to use my eyes to pass some of my classes. Worse yet, I couldn't even sleep in class. Sleeping in class was one of my favorite high school pastimes. I even brought a pillow to my high school physics class to avoid getting unfashionable desk imprints on my forehead, but at the Academy, sleeping equaled demerits and demerits meant no social life. Of course, threatening to take away your social life at the USAF Academy was kind of like threatening to take away driving privileges from a two-year old.

Not being one to sit around and be abused by bad genes, I decided to take whatever steps were necessary to salvage the unfair hand dealt to me by my insensitive parents. The first action I took was to acquire a book on restoring perfect vision to malfunctioning eyes. Why were all these people in the world wearing glasses and contacts? All they had to do was follow the simple instructions in this book, including the chapter on the benefits of staring directly at the sun (no kidding), and no longer would they need those cumbersome instruments of vision correction— they could trade their glasses and contacts in for a cane and a German Shepherd. My results were less than stellar, but on the upside, at least I quit staring at the sun before I went blind.

Giving up on that sort of modern day witchcraft, I decided to take a less ambiguous route and attack my eyes directly. The trauma I was to suffer in the ensuing months would prepare me well for my career in the Air Force, that is, if my career included being shot down, captured, and then tortured by having my eyes sliced open and salt dumped in them.

The instrument of destruction I chose is called Orthokerotonomy. The way Ortho-K (as we veterans call it) works is to put specially made contact lenses in your eyes. These contact lenses appear to be the same as ordinary contact lenses. The only subtle difference you might notice while wearing them is that, while driving, you may find yourself seriously considering a head-on with a Mack truck just to relieve the agony.

The Ortho-K lenses are designed to smash the cornea flat, thereby curing nearsightedness, but also inducing insanity. I used to enjoy sleeping through classes in high school. With these lenses in place, sleeping in class was not even a distant dream. Sitting there with my eyes swollen and bloodshot, all I could think about was the bell ending each session. Between classes, I would sprint to the bathroom, eject the lenses, savor blessed relief for a moment, and then reinstall the contacts for the next class. Seven classes a day, five days a week, this scenario was repeated for the remainder of my freshman year and throughout my sophomore year.

Sometimes my eyes were so swollen I couldn't pop the lenses out by the normal method. For these extreme cases, I carried a small plunger. The plunger was supposed to latch onto the lens, allowing the user to pull it out of his eye. This method worked great, except for one time when, unbeknownst to me, my contact had slid off to the side of my eye. Already wincing in agony, I hastily pushed the plunger into my eye. With it firmly attached, I began to pull—pull my eyeball out, that is. The plunger was attached, not to the wayward lens, but directly to my eye. It's still kind of painful just remembering these sorts of incidents in life.

Although I was unable to sleep in class with the contacts in my eyes, that didn't prevent me from finding myself in trouble. I was accused of the very activity that I longed for, but could not participate in. Once, while sitting in the back of a mechanical engineering class, writhing in particularly intense pain, the teacher took notice of me. My eyes were almost shut from swelling. Seeing the narrow slits from which I peered, he warned me not to fall asleep in HIS class. There is no justice in life.

I managed to squint and squirm through two years of shear torture, courtesy of the Ortho-K profession. The only relief came during the summers. Suffering at the Academy was one thing—that was expected whether I wore the lenses or not—but suffering while away on my meager vacations was out of the question. Wearing the lenses would destroy what little rest and relaxation I had, so during the summer, my lenses remained safely tucked away in their little containers. My eyes appreciated the break and returned to their previously warped state. They also shed the inch thick calluses that had formed on their corneas as a defense against assault by the Ortho-K lenses.

During the summer between my sophomore and junior years, while attending the U.S. Army Airborne Jump School, I acquired my first car—a 1968 Camaro convertible. The Camaro was well received when I returned to Virginia, especially by the police. However, they didn't seem to appreciate the finer points of my well-honed driving techniques.

I hadn't worn the Ortho-K lenses the entire time I was on my summer break, but I decided to wear the lenses for the long journey back to Colorado. During the 2,000 mile drive to the Academy, my technique was simple: Never, ever, under any circumstances, allow another car to pass. If another car passed, that meant I was driving too slowly.

I discovered that I wouldn't notice the agony caused by the contacts when I was sufficiently distracted (working out, driving at 100 mph, open heart surgery, etc.). My high speed, nonstop (except when I plowed into a guardrail) drive back to the Academy gave me plenty of distractions to keep my mind off of the contacts; this was not a good thing. It's similar to taking a Caribbean vacation on the very last day of winter when you're at your whitest, skipping the suntan lotion and spending the entire trip lying out in the sun, although much more painful.

An indication that something was amiss occurred after I removed the lenses for the first time in 14 hours. I was spending the night in the best motel I could find for about 10 dollars. I looked around and noticed that a thick fog had descended over the entire countryside, including that part of the countryside between the TV and my bed. "I'll just sleep it off," I thought, and I did, until about two a.m. At that time, I sat up and tried to open my eyes; I couldn't. The reason I couldn't was because there was a four inch knife penetrating each of my eyelids and running straight through my eyeballs, or maybe someone had melted my eyelids to my eyeballs with hot coals. I wasn't sure, but I really, really needed to drench my eyes in water, NOW!

I threw on my bathing suit and dove into the swimming pool that was just outside of my door. It was then that I realized that chlorine and serrated eyes are not a good combination. Fortunately, my underwater screams did not disturb the other guests. I crawled back into bed, only able to lie there with my eyes half closed.

The next day I arose to continue my drive to the Academy with one minor obstacle to overcome—I couldn't see. Lucky for pedestrians, I could tell the difference between the road and a sidewalk, but when it came to other, less distinguished features, such as which side of the road I should be on, curves in the road, etc., I was clueless. On my way out I sat, perplexed, directly in front of a traffic light, unable to discern if it was red or green. Finally, I eased into the intersection, checking both ways for any giant blobs moving in my direction, and continued on my way.

After many close calls on the way back to Colorado, my Camaro and I finally crept into the Academy parking lot. The next day, I was surprised to find that I could see 20/20! I had perfect vision! Of course, the scar tissue left by the Ortho-K lenses would leave me blind by the time I hit 50, but I didn't care. I was increasing my chances of getting into pilot training!

Unfortunately, I had to discontinue wearing the contacts because of my dear stepmother, the federal government. The powers that be decided to ban cadets from using Ortho-K lenses. If you ask me, they were being awfully picky. Apparently, some complaints from pilot training bases were finding their way back to the Academy. Cadets who had used the lenses to gain entry into pilot training decided that, now that their goal was achieved, there was no need to wear the lenses any longer.

Having experienced firsthand the agony inducing capacity of Ortho-K lenses, I could hardly blame those guys. However, some of them started out with vision close to 20/3000. Without the lenses, their eyes returned to an earlier deformed condition. Obviously, these nitpicky Air Force types wanted us to be able to see before *and* after our final eye exam. Some people are never satisfied. I suppose seeing far enough to know if your visor is up or down while flying in three-foot fingertip formation at 400 mph and landing at 200 mph might help the students' performance a little.

Instructor: "Nice formation flight, Joe.
You got a little close to lead though."

Joe: "We were flying formation?"

Denied the privilege of suffering for two more years under the auspices of my contact lenses, I reverted to my patented "graduate without reading" program. In an effort to reduce my reading workload, I chose astronautical engineering as my major. Astronautical engineering was known as the second most difficult major at the Academy, the most difficult being "How to Have a Social Life" with the minor "How to Find Women: They do Exist!"

Why would I choose a major so exciting that I declared publicly, "If I ever use this major to make a living, I'll shoot myself?" The answer is, in all seriousness, reading. To learn history, lots of reading is required, likewise with English, management, you name it. However, with a technical subject, all that is needed is to grasp the concepts. Grasping concepts should take only a minute or two, right? Luckily, no one was around to remind me of this rationale as I stared for endless hours at the lime green letters on a computer monitor, writing programs for a manned mission to Mars, tracking satellites, or my personal favorite, firing nukes at the Soviet Union.

Yes, I could have gone blind working in front of that computer. Worse, I could have become a bonafide, certifiable geek. What were the effects of soaking for two endless years in this spa of geekdom? At least the Academy had a test to see how our eyes endured, but what of our social skills? They were perhaps lost forever, if they ever existed at all.

Of course, there was no sense in worrying about social skills that I would never need once I entered the "real" Air Force. It was rumored that half of the assignments given out at pilot training would be to the dreaded Northern Tier. Basically, all of the Northern Tier assignments in the Air Force are located north of the North Pole, only with fewer women. So, robbing us of any of our remaining social skills was not only a less than challenging task for the administrators at the Academy, it was also a meaningless gesture, since those skills didn't have a snowball's chance in you know what of being used.

Still, pilot training for us cadets was the Holy Grail. We just HAD to get there and succeed. Without any further techniques for eye preservation available to me, I relied on the three weeks prior to my entry into Undergraduate Pilot Training (UPT) at Columbus AFB, Mississippi, to provide them with the needed rest before the big exam. For those three weeks, I was assigned to the Military Police (MPs). I don't remember much about the work I did in that interim period. In fact, all I can remember is playing tennis and water skiing on the river with the boat my roommate and I purchased just as soon as we arrived. I suppose my eyes got as much rest as could be expected when a 21-year old is released from captivity for the first time in four years.

At last, the test came. There should have been the quintessential drum roll as I stepped up for my turn to read the eye chart. This was my true final exam before I was qualified to enter UPT. Four years of worry and agony summed up in this one moment. And.......

I couldn't read all of the letters on the line! I could make out only one or two. I tried all the techniques in my arsenal: the twisting, the squinting, but no way was I going to read them all. Goodbye, fighter jets, I was history. Then, I noticed that the administrator was looking at me with that, "You moron" look I'm so familiar with seeing. "That's the 20/15 line," he said. Yes! Requiring only a slight squint, I was able to read the 20/20 line above it. The entire episode was so brief and unceremonious that I could hardly believe it. That was all. My journey was complete. No more worries about my eyes. Once the Air Force had sunk a million dollars into my training, I was home free. I could go blind, but they could never get rid of me now!

Little did I know that my battle had just begun against the eyes my parents had given me. No longer would the Air Force Medical Hobby Shop (as we referred to the flight surgeons and their hospitals) be standing in the way of my dreams, now it would be evil airline personnel departments and the elusive standards of their medical examinations that would be my nemesis.

At this point, I had yet to hear about the airlines, but I was soon to find out. Shortly after I walked into the KC-10 squadron at Barksdale AFB, Louisiana, I understood why it was referred to as "airline lead-in school." Almost everyone below the rank of colonel had just one thing on their minds: to be hired by a major airline. Everything revolved around this goal—how the flying time was divided, who went on night flights, and who could grab the trips with the most hours in the air. Most of the guys were members of Future Airline Pilots of America (FAPA), an organization with a monthly magazine that told how many, who, and why the airlines were hiring, not to mention the salaries. Of course, no one was leaving the Air Force for "the money" in the airlines; at least no one would admit to it. That would be greedy. When asked, "So, why are you going to the airlines?" The answer was never "money." The usual response was, "for the lifestyle," which, of course, has nothing to do with money.

> Me: "Are you going to the airlines?"
>
> Fellow Pilot: "Yep, I'm gonna take my wife and the kids and move into a brand new trailer park just as soon as I get hired. Now that's a step up in lifestyle."
>
> Me: "Why don't you use some of that fat salary and buy a big ol' house?"
>
> Fellow Pilot: "Because I'm not going to the airlines for the money."

We even had a complementary airline interview library, complete with books stuffed full of notes from every interview since the Wright brothers flew at Kitty Hawk. There were even memorized copies of some tests given by a few companies, in addition to the "approved solutions" for questionnaires like the MMPI psychobabble test, complete with stern warnings of impending failure if the tester failed to meet the required psychological profile: gullible and naïve.

Sample MMPI question:
"Do people lie, steal and cheat?"

Answer: "No."
Evaluation: The subject is well
    adjusted and stable.

Answer: "Yes."
Evaluation: Don't hire this
    misanthropic scum.

As I studied all of the information at my disposal, it became obvious that being hired by a major airline required nothing more than the body of Hercules, the mind of Einstein, the wisdom of Solomon, and the flying ability of Superman. After achieving the body of Hercules, only more muscular, I began working on the Einstein thing. However, deep down, I knew my vision still had to survive my six remaining years in the Air Force. I turned to Dr. Mary.

Several pilots had gone to Dr. Mary to correct their less-than-perfect vision. She assured me that by wearing the glasses she prescribed and performing the necessary exercises, my eyes would return to 20/20. As she sat there across from me, wearing trifocals, her eyes looking the size of grapefruits, the obvious irony never seemed to occur to her. I was back to voodoo, and my mentor was Witchdoctor Mary. The results were surprisingly phenomenal—for Dr. Mary's bank account.

The first item on Dr. Mary's list was to fit me with a new pair of glasses. The pair I currently owned had a prescription that was "entirely too powerful." "Entirely too powerful" defined as, "You can actually see something." The new pair of glasses Dr. Mary prescribed did three things. First, and most important, the glasses enabled a substantial transfer of wealth from me to Dr. Mary. Second, for distance vision, the glasses eliminated my ability to see anything further than 10 feet. As Dr. Mary explained, "You don't want your eyes to become dependent on glasses." Of course, how silly of me! Why had I been wearing glasses that worked, if I wanted to get rid of them in the first place? Third, for near vision, Dr. Mary equipped my glasses with the small reading segment like you see 90-year olds using. These segments transformed the clarity of my near vision into exactly the same clarity the glasses gave me for distant vision, or in other words, none. Personally, I think eye patches would have been a cheaper, one-size-fits-all alternative to these glasses.

Slowly, the picture was beginning to come into focus, but that was the only thing coming into focus. Dr. Mary was trying to implement my own patented method developed at the USAF Academy. Outside of her office, she didn't want me to use my eyes for anything, at least not for seeing. However, inside her office, Dr. Mary implemented a different plan. She had me strapped to various machines that took my eyes through a plethora of "exercises" designed to turn each of them into little Arnold Schwarzeneggers. These little Arnolds were supposed to force my eyes into seeing better, whether they liked it or not.

Unfortunately, for some reason unknown to accomplished scientists like Dr. Mary, my eyes refused to improve. However, one thing did improve—Dr. Mary's ability to evade my questions as to why she wore glasses as thick as a window on a submarine. Why didn't she just use her own tried-and-true techniques? After all of the cash she collected from shmucks like me, she could certainly afford to pay for the treatment. When I posed any sort of question of this nature, I experienced the distinct feeling that I was treading on forbidden ground. I was in the empress's court, she had no clothes (yuck!), and I was rude enough to point out that fact.

Fortunately for me, I was granted a pardon each time I made an inquiry—a pardon in the form of a lengthy stare from Dr. Mary's enormous tarantula-like eyes—and then, ignoring those inquiries completely, the empress would pretend that nothing had ever been said. We would press on to more important matters, such as the next and more expensive phase of my treatment.

After being relieved of hundreds of dollars, I gave up on Dr. Mary and all of her methods, except for the tried-and-true no reading technique that was the essence of Dr. Mary's plan anyway, only I could do that one far cheaper myself. It was tough, but I stuck to a disciplined routine of no reading, extra sleep, and plenty of television.

Confidently, I approached the impending airline interview process, certain that I could squeak by. Then, I heard about THE FORM. Every airline was going to require each candidate to sign THE FORM. This form was concerned with just one topic: Ortho-K. Wouldn't you know it, just like the Air Force, the airlines also wanted their pilots to be able to see and not just for the interview.

Each company's form was worded only slightly differently than this:

I, the undersigned, swear on the graves of my forefathers and foremothers that I have never, ever, ever been closer than two miles to an Ortho-K lens in my entire life and three subsequent past lives, and I certainly have never put one in my eyes. If I am found to be lying about any part of the above statement, I am liable for this action and may have my eyes removed by the Company for further examination. In addition, I acknowledge that there will be no way for at least one century that my application will pass any further with the Company, except to be used in a certain capacity in the washroom.

Sign Here_____

I hadn't worn an Ortho-K lens in almost a decade. How could I prove that I hadn't? Easy, I had evidence. I had passed the psychology test. If I passed the psychology test, I must be mostly sane, and if I am sane, then I couldn't have been wearing those lenses for the past 10 years; no person could without serious mental consequences.

No, no. That wouldn't be good enough. I had to sign this form or no airline job. As I conferred over this dilemma with a fellow pilot, he began to sing the theme song from the local truck driving school, as though that's where I was headed. "When you drive a truck....."

I began to rationalize. "C'mon, after 10 years, my eyes have no lasting effect from those lenses. I can sign the form." The choices were laid clearly out in front of me. I could sign the form and have a multimillion dollar career with a major airline, or I could be honest, write an explanation to the company, and start working on my truck driving skills. Here was my moral dilemma, or as Homer Simpson once put it, "Mora whata?" However, I'm not Homer; I just couldn't sign the form. Curse you, conscience! I wrote my explanation and left the interview depressed and far more anxious than when I had arrived.

However, there was the happy ending. I was hired, which is why I nearly shattered the eardrum of the lady who gave me the good news. How have my eyes done since then? I don't want to imply that I've let my eyes go since that fateful day many years ago, but I'd say that they've fared about as well as my cholesterol. Yes, we also had to pass a stringent cholesterol test. As a precaution, months before the interview, I cut all fat out of my diet. Unfortunately, I can't tell you what my cholesterol is today. It must have been fine back then, but approximately 300 gallons of Haagen Dazs and 600 pounds of chocolate later, who knows? I've never had it checked. Why should I? I've won life's lottery.

Coming Clean

I'd like to take this opportunity to announce my candidacy for the office of President of the United States. I meet all of the requirements at least as well as my opponents do: natural born citizenship, age, and pulse. Voters might expect that now would be a good time to explain to the American people why they should cast their vote for me. Do I have positions on all of the important issues of today? The answer is...Yes!

Undoubtedly, by taking such a hard stance, about half of all Americans are standing on their chairs, cheering and already hoping for my second term. The other half is planning protests, riots, and assassination. Also, seeing me for the potent enemy that I am, about now, my opponents are digging into my past in an attempt to uncover any sordid events that may have occurred, or to fabricate those events as necessary.

Therefore, I have decided to do some damage control by revealing everything in my past that could be

31

used against me, and then, in good political form, denying that any of it ever occurred.

I think it is best to start with the Burpee flower seeds, or as my opponents would call it: my involvement in "organized crime with the intention of bankrupting the great American flower seed industry."

It's true. In my past, I have possessed numerous unused and unpaid for packages of Burpee flower seeds, ordered from a form available on the back of any Spiderman comic book. The flower seed ads were adjacent to the ones selling X-ray glasses, which *I* never purchased, but I have *heard* that each of my opponents has. They still wear them while campaigning (ladies, beware!).

Sometime during the fifth grade, I decided to get rich selling Burpee seeds to my neighbors, but mainly to my mom. I was certain she would feel obligated to purchase any unsold packages. As I recall, I spent at least one long summer afternoon attempting to peddle the seeds the Burpee company had sent me. Unfortunately, after thirty minutes of going all out, I had not one sale to show for my efforts. My own attempts to grow the flowers had similarly dismal results.

Soon, the first bill from the Burpee company arrived. They claimed that I owed them some astronomical sum of money. The total bill exceeded my net worth many times over; it was probably about ten dollars. Where was I supposed to come up with that kind of money? Don't answer, "Sell the seeds." I had already maxed out that effort weeks before during that one afternoon.

I decided to handle the bill the next best way to actually paying it—I buried it deep in the kitchen garbage, ensuring no parents' eyes would ever have a chance to cast a gaze upon it. With the bill problem solved, I went on dreaming up other moneymaking schemes. Then, the second notice arrived. This bill had large letters and threatened to ruin my credit for life if payment wasn't promptly submitted. My future purchases of a car, home, and more importantly, candy were in jeopardy.

Shortly, a third bill arrived. The third bill mentioned something about destroying my reputation and said, "Don't you ever even THINK about running for president."

There you have it. I've come clean on the Burpee seed scandal. I don't know how the Burpee company ever recovered from my abuse of the system, but let me say here and now, that when elected president, if the Burpee company will just forget that little bill from 1973, they can count on me for a big fat subsidy at the taxpayers' expense.

Another "scandal" my opponents might dredge up is one they would label as "misuse of public funds." The "public funds" they would be referring to was the money I collected around my neighborhood under a category I labeled as the "Library Fund."

My idea was to raise enough cash to make certain that Laurel Ridge Elementary School in Fairfax, Virginia would pay our librarian whatever it took to ensure that she never left our school. At this point in my life, I don't think I quite understood the concept of death (which from the looks of the frail, elderly woman was a more likely possibility than that of her ever being fired).

The reason I wanted to keep our librarian around was for the horror stories she told us. Even though I am a chicken at heart when it comes to things like scary movies, I couldn't wait for the days when all the students would be released from class to gather around her as she spun another yarn. There were vampires, ghosts, giant spiders, and human body parts that sought out fresh victims. What I wouldn't give to go back and observe the looks on our faces—looks that could only mean, "I'm not going to sleep for a week!" I was hooked on her tales like an addict, and I didn't want to see my supply cut off.

My fundraising efforts were going just fine until I came to a certain house that contained a ferocious dog that weighed at least five pounds. Just as soon as a crack in the door appeared, the dog lunged for me. The owner pried his (the dog's) mouth off of my outstretched hand, and for some reason, made a sizable donation to my burgeoning Library Fund. Valuing my blood and random body parts, I decided to end any further collection efforts.

Whatever happened to the funds I collected? Investigations would prove that not even one cent of the money ever made it to the Laurel Ridge Elementary School library. I say just chalk the whole thing up to "bureaucratic red tape." Also, since none of the donations ever left my possession, technically, the money does not qualify as "public funds." The paltry sum I retained was used to comfort me after my near-death experience and to aid in my recovery by purchasing Toasted Almond or Strawberry Shortcake ice cream bars from the Good Humor Man that summer.

Finally, my opponents may try to tarnish my name by accusing me of being involved in "gang-related activities." This accusation is, of course, totally false, unless being a member and leader of a gang can somehow be twisted around into the appearance of guilt.

My stint as a gang leader took place in the third grade at Garden Hills Elementary School in Atlanta, Georgia. The third grade at Garden Hills had three gangs—two American and one Cuban. Our gangs were just like any other gangs you might think of, except for the knives, guns, drugs, and crime. What we did do was fight. Our fights occurred almost every day during recess.

I remember our diminutive teacher, and believe me, if *I* thought she was small, she was definitely a runt. I only weighed 45 pounds myself (probably the smallest boy in class), so I think I had a reasonable perspective on being small. Our teacher would stand near the top of our playground, clearly able to see the fights that broke out, but she never made a single attempt to stop any of it. I can't say that I blame her. At her size, intervention might have proved dangerous.

How I ever ended up as one of the American gang leaders, I will never know. Just the year before, my mother, two brothers, and I had moved to Atlanta to be near my grandparents while my father was away in Vietnam. I felt like a total misfit and outcast. Now, in the third grade, I had risen to gang leader.

I remember several of the fights that I had. One was against the other American gang leader. I won. In fact, I always won, otherwise I could not have remained our gang's leader. However, there was one opponent that I made every effort to avoid. In the Cuban gang, there was a kid named Fernando that was easily over twice my size. He wasn't their gang's leader, but he was their ace in the hole, sort of like Robin Hood's Little John (Little Juan, in this case). Through strategic planning, I made sure I kept away from anything that might cause a confrontation with that behemoth.

A Cuban kid named Nicky was our translator. He was fluent in both English and Spanish—a real novelty to us back in 1971. Nicky wasn't part of any gang, and on the side, I considered him my friend. Our gangs didn't mingle during recess, but Nicky would drift back and forth between the groups and tell us what was going on in each gang.

In my gang, there were several athletic guys who I wasn't really sure I could take in a fight. They were bigger and faster than I was, but they never challenged me. Two of these guys were named Mike and Steve.

As I approached the field during recess on one fateful day, I saw a sight that made my heart skip a beat— for about 20 seconds. My sphincter didn't hold up so well, either. Mike and Steve were running circles around Fernando. First, Mike would swoop in and tap Fernando on his head, and then, Steve would follow up with a tap of his own.

It looked similar to the scene in King Kong when the biplanes were pestering Kong as he stood atop of the Empire State Building. This was a situation I had spent most of the third grade trying to avoid. All of a sudden, just as I feared, like Kong in the movie, Fernando timed his punch perfectly. He caught Mike square in the face. Fernando wasn't quick, but he was powerful. Mike dropped to the ground, grasping his newly flattened nose. My worst nightmare had happened.

By the unwritten Code of Gangs, I was now required to face off with Fernando. He had taken out one of my guys. I had no choice but to even the score or die trying. The die trying part was the section of the code that bothered me. I didn't see any way I was going to take Fernando. No way could I take him down, and I knew he would laugh at my feeble attempts at punching him. Nonetheless, all eyes turned to me, as I, David, strode up to meet my Goliath.

A ring of onlookers encircled us. Nicky strategically placed himself inside the ring and between the two fighters—our self-appointed referee. Quickly, I formulated my strategy. I was going to wear Fernando out. To an untrained observer, it may have appeared that I was backing up just to stay out of range of Fernando's meaty fists. No way! That would have been cowardly. I just figured that, if I could keep this retreat up long enough, maybe Fernando would tire out, at which point I could take him, or perhaps recess would end and we could forget the whole thing.

I raised my fists ready to fight, and then I started to back up. Emboldened by the quick dispatch of my fellow gang member and ready to finish up by squashing me like a little insect, Fernando moved forward. The situation looked good for the first three or four yards of my retreat. Then, Fernando began to say things. Fortunately, since it was all in Spanish, I couldn't understand a word of it. Ever louder, Fernando continued spewing forth his Spanish diatribe. I should have left well enough alone, but instead I asked Nicky, "What's he saying?"

"He says, 'Why do you keep backing up, are you chicken?'" Nicky replied. I *had* to ask! Now what was I going to do? Everybody had heard it. I keep backing up, and I'm a chicken. Some people just don't appreciate good strategy.

I paused, tightened my fist, and did something I had never considered doing since laying eyes on Fernando—I stepped forward. With all the strength I could muster, I punched him straight in the gut. It felt as though half of my arm disappeared in his layers of fat. As I retracted my fist, I took half a step back to ascertain the success of my assault.

Nothing. I had to admit; it certainly felt like I hadn't done any damage, and indeed, I hadn't. I looked at Fernando's expressionless face. "Boy, am I going to take a pounding now," I thought. Then, like a sheet of ice falling from a glacier, Fernando's face cracked and contorted. Tears burst forth as he grasped his stomach and collapsed to the ground. All at once, a cheer went up and my gang hoisted me on their shoulders, whisking me away (thank goodness). I had dropped Fernando with one punch that had inadvertently connected with his solar plexus.

So, there you have it—all of the questionable activities in my past. None of this ever occurred, of course, so remember—write me in on the ballot at the next election.

Junk Food

I have something to confess. I have an affliction. However, I'm sorry to disappoint those of you who find satisfaction in the difficulties of others. Most people would probably consider my affliction to be an asset. The fact is, I can't gain weight. Believe me, I've tried. I doubt you could find a dietician who wouldn't cringe when observing the plethora of unhealthy foods I ingest each day. It's possible that I'm rotting from the inside out, but it's a difficult process finding the motivation to change one's habits without any visible reason to do so. A bunch of nebulous numbers associated with terms such as "cholesterol" or "blood pressure" are hardly a motivating factor when it comes to giving up life sustaining foods that fall into categories like "dessert" or "snack."

It is not that I try to be unhealthy. It's just an instinctive feeling that I'll slowly starve to death if I don't consume my Minimum Daily Calorie Allowance (MDCA), which happens to be somewhere around 5,000. A friend of mine, who gains weight just by giving food a lengthy stare, reminded me of a time when we dropped into a convenience store. Seeing how carefully I was mulling over each candy bar on the aisle, he inquired as to what I was doing. "I'm looking for the one with the most calories," I responded. Understandably, this revelation didn't go over well with my weight watching companion.

I don't consume fat laden foods just to be disgusting; it's truly a matter of maintaining my current weight. However, today, it appears most Americans are trying to lose weight, or at least they should be. Working on a more svelte figure would have been a noble goal for a Boy Scout I knew in the high school. Ronny was already sporting a sizable beer gut by the ninth grade. Genuine hunger pangs were probably not a usual part of his daily experience. He was the kind of kid whose mom must have packed his lunch with two sodas and an extra dessert.

On this particular day, we were riding in the rear of a military deuce-and-a-half truck on our way back from a Boy Scout camp out. The leftover food from the trip was stored next to us in the back of the truck. Alan, a friend of mine, being the troublemaker he was, pointed to an unopened stick of margarine, and said to Ronny, "I bet you can't eat that entire stick of butter."

Ronny responded, "Give me five dollars and I will."

"Okay," Alan retorted.

Watching our fellow camper avidly bite into the slimy, smarmy glob of margarine would make anyone's stomach groan with nausea. It was disgusting!

I knew for a fact that Alan didn't have the five bucks to cover the bet. That fact didn't seem to occur to him. Also, Alan was, literally, just half the size of this other kid. As Ronny forced down the rest of the treat, he demanded his five bucks. "Forget it, I'm not paying you," Alan laughed. Ronny most likely would have tried to strangle Alan on the spot, but after downing his afternoon snack, I suspect he didn't feel quite up to the task.

I was never able to maintain extra tonnage like Ronny. I also had no intention of consuming raw sticks of butter in an effort to do so, but a few items have forced their way into my diet, ensuring that I won't face death by starvation. One of these items is the banana.

There was a time when I wouldn't touch a banana. In fact, a while back, I would have turned a blind eye if there was imprisonment for moms who successfully suckered a kid into believing he was about to eat vanilla pudding, only to discover after the first bite that it was infested with bananas. This deception ranks right up with the chicanery of serving cookies that look exactly like fresh, homemade chocolate chip, when in reality, they're oatmeal cookies laced with raisins. In my opinion, both of these offenses border on child abuse. If a proper, multimillion dollar government study were conducted on the inherent dangers to a child whose taste buds are primed for a delectable, sugar-filled, fat-laden snack, only to bite into some semi-healthy junk food substitute, it would undoubtedly conclude that the child suffers heinous and irreparable damage.

Although bananas have slithered their way into my diet, other "foods," such as beets, caraway seeds, and cottage cheese, I staunchly refuse to touch. These grotesque mutants of nature should come with mandatory warning labels to preclude their use by unsuspecting humans. At least in the case of beets or a curdled mass of cottage cheese, any normal person can gaze at them and deduce immediately that these are not meant for internal consumption. The caraway seed is a far more devious foe. I'll never forget my first run-in with caraway seeds. It was in the third grade. I had been out with a friend participating in the usual random destruction of our neighborhood. Exhausted from our labors, he invited me over to his place to relax and grab a snack. His mom presented us with ordinary looking peanut butter sandwiches. I was famished, and immediately scarfed down half of the sandwich in a couple of bites.

It is a bit reckless to consume food more rapidly than your taste buds can relay pertinent data to your brain. No doubt, my taste buds were screaming a neurological SOS to mine. It probably went something like this:

"You idiot! That sandwich you're
eating is poisonous.

It's contaminated with caraway seeds.

Now your only options are:

1. Go to the nearest toilet
   and induce vomiting or

2. Gargle liberally with Clorox"

As usual, my taste buds had faithfully delivered a precise and accurate analysis of the situation. In spite of having to endure this deep distress, I maintained my composure, excused myself, and gracefully flushed the remaining portion of the sandwich down my host's commode. The aftertaste lingered for only a week or two, and thankfully, my mouth experienced a complete recovery. My ability to recoup was probably due to youth and the diminutive amount of caraway seeds actually consumed. I am certain that if it had been a beet or cottage cheese sandwich, it would have done me in for sure.

Some readers might wonder why I didn't attempt to wash down that bite of sandwich with a soda. Although the caraway seeds would have made it into my body, at least the soda could have covered up the taste, in addition to adding to the overall calorie count of the meal. Both of these points are valid. The problem is, as much as I am dedicated to all forms of junk food, I am not a soda drinker.

One reason I don't care too much for soda is that, when I was a youngster, my parents wouldn't allow me to indulge in the finer things in life, such as coffee, soda, or liquor, not to mention, smoking and drugs. I still pretty much avoid all of those habits today, including the sodas. My most notable vices have long been candy bars and ice cream. The evolution of this condition, as with most people, is two-fold. One part is due to heredity, and the second to environment.

The heredity part is evident in the primal urge drawing me to any chocolate or ice cream that isn't secured in an air tight vault with steel walls at least two feet thick (note: I've probably consumed a pound or two of chocolate while editing this story).

The environmental part of the equation stems from money, or rather, the lack of money at my disposal during my formative years. As a child, when I rifled with great hope through my pockets, I would usually find that I was faced with the unjust choice of spending my meager allowance on either a soda or a candy bar. There was never enough dinero for both. I could either drink water and eat a candy bar, or just drink a soda. The choice was clear. I always needed to experience some chewing action to achieve a bearable level of satisfaction. Of the two possibilities, only the candy bar could provide both sustenance and the necessary physical interaction needed to achieve total gratification.

This weakness for candy and ice cream has bankrupted me more than once in my life. If all the experts I read these days are correct about the deleterious effects of consuming extra sugar and fat, junk food may bankrupt me yet again. The first time I recall having a load of money and discovering that I blew the whole shebang on chocolate and ice cream was the summer between fifth and sixth grade. I had what I believed to be a limitless amount of savings in my favorite Buckingham Palace Soldier piggy bank. I'm not sure where all the money came from, but I thought it would never run out, sort of the way most Americans view using credit cards these days. Well, that summer, the Piggy Bank God failed me.

Every day the Good Humor Man would drive down the cul-de-sac in front of my house, and in a trance-like state, I would go to my piggy bank, remove the necessary funds, and pay homage to this deity in white. My preferred sacrifices were the Strawberry Shortcake and the Toasted Almond ice cream bars. I hardly missed a day with the Good Humor Man that summer, but near the end of the season, I made the traditional journey to my bank, carefully unlocked the latch, and found it barren. I was horrified, and for a moment, was sure I'd been robbed, no doubt by one of my untrustworthy brothers. I quickly ruled out that possibility though, because of how meticulously I had locked my piggy bank each day—after robbing it myself. I had to face the truth. I had eaten through my entire life's savings, years of hard work, and now, not a penny to show for it. I vowed that I would never be so foolish again, and perhaps thus far I haven't been, but there have been several times when, out of nostalgia, I go to the grocery store and buy a six pack—of Good Humor bars that is—and consume the entire contents in one sitting. Believe me, it isn't easy. It has taken me a lifetime to develop this precise level of self-control.

Today, my dietary intake is no longer at the whim of a buddy's mother or a grossly insubstantial allowance. As a commercial pilot, I consider myself privileged in that I am able to consume enormous amounts of airline food. I've heard all the complaints about how inedible airline "food" is. Let me tell you, eating airline food, including the omelets, is like dining in the finest French restaurants compared to the box lunches we Air Force crew members were forced to consume.

During my time commanding the KC-10 Extender, box lunches were issued to us by the base kitchens before we launched on our missions. These lunches were always cold and usually contained, amongst other tasteless items, a sandwich with an unidentifiable meaty substance. The lunches always had a usable "life" of just a few hours imprinted on the side of the box, which usually expired sometime during the middle of our sortie. If you didn't shut your eyes and consume the wretched contents immediately, odds were that when you had enough time to eat lunch during the mission, your box's "life" had expired and you were on your own—eat at your own risk. Faced with the possibility of starvation on one hand and food poisoning on the other, I usually opted for my longtime favorite: the no-sandwich box lunch.

The no-sandwich box lunch was a culinary delight consisting of several Twinkies or Ding-Dongs, assorted candy bars, and a couple of Cokes—the true warrior's diet. What's more, its expiration date was sometime in the next millennium. There was no more worrying about food poisoning or the cook sneezing on the entrée. The only downside would be the slightly elevated blood sugar levels induced by consuming basically one item from the four food groups. This condition might cause a pilot who consumed a no-sandwich box lunch to shake and twitch nervously. An additional side effect of the no-sandwich box lunch was that the pilot's nervousness might transfer to other members of the crew, if that pilot were flying the aircraft in one of the more "critical" phases of flight, such as the landing.

I like to believe that, through a disciplined regime of consistently consuming the no-sandwich box lunch, I sort of built up an immunity to any of its side effects. As evidence to support this claim, I submit one incident that occurred during my unit's deployment as part of Operation Desert Shield. The KC-10's were being flown 24 hours a day, bringing supplies to our troops in Saudi Arabia. One mission that I personally commanded was to deliver a plane full of tampons. This load was an emergency shipment caused by the Army's minor oversight concerning the special needs of some of their newer combat troops.

Our jets started in the U.S., refueled in Spain, and then flew on to Saudi Arabia. My group was tasked to fly the leg from Spain into Saudi Arabia. On one particular day, when our aircraft arrived from the States, instead of the usual quick turn (that is taking off within the hour of the plane's arrival) we sat on the ground for three hours due to a mechanical problem.

Fortunately, as most units do, our operations kept a refrigerator stocked with pay-as-you-go goodies. There were assorted soft drinks and candy bars with a money jar in which to place your coins after you made a selection. As could accurately be predicted, I always opted for the candy bars. Here's where my innovative and patented method for developing total resistance to any side effects of consuming a no-sandwich box lunch met its first live test in the field.

There I was, stranded on the ramp at Zaragoza Air Base, Spain, with a broken KC-10. With three hours before the aircraft would be ready to get airborne, but not knowing at the time how long we would actually have to wait, I moseyed back to operations for a light snack, a P.B. Max bar. P.B. Max bars have peanut butter, chocolate, and a cookie - calories to the max. I threw some change in the money jar, took my candy bar, and went to play my 114th game of computer golf. After a while, maybe 10 minutes, I went back to stock up again before I starved to death. By the time we were informed that our aircraft was ready, I had repeated this scenario NINE times. I only quit because the frig, in another example of poor military planning, ran out of P.B. Max bars. I certainly wasn't the limiting factor in this case. My stomach was more than ready to partake of yet another delicious treat. My money supply wasn't a limiting factor either. I was ready to break a twenty to keep the candy bars coming. The strangest part of it all was that I felt no side effects whatsoever from ingesting those candy bars.

During the flight, I never experienced a sugar high or let down, and I slept like a baby on my break. I felt so normal that it kind of scared me. Now I realize that this was a true testament to an acquired resistance to anything a no-sandwich box lunch could ever throw at me. All military personnel should be required to satisfactorily complete such training. It's time to adopt my innovative program, before we're caught unprepared in the next conflict and find our troops vulnerable to enemy chocolate bars.

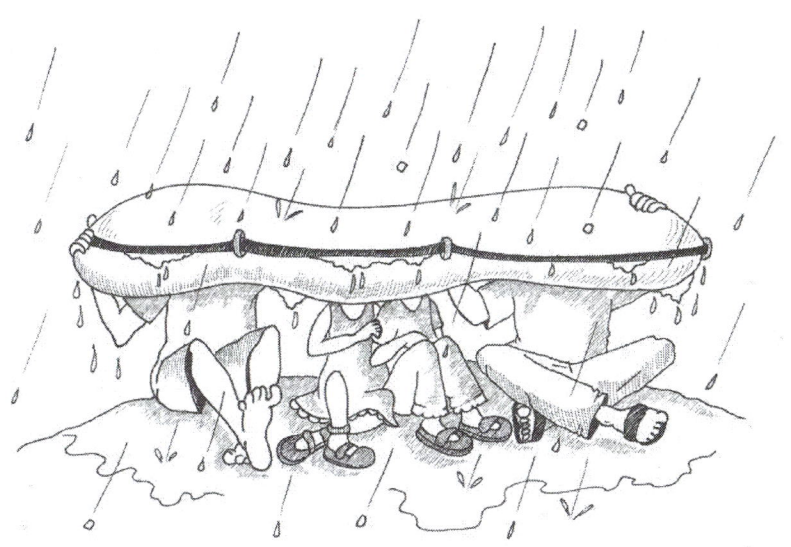

Rescue?

In our family, as in all families, there are subtle, but recognizable differences between siblings. Subtle differences like that between the Wright Flyer and the space shuttle, or between Curly and Einstein, or between cheeses, like cheddar and cottage. Cheddar cheese is delicious, whereas cottage cheese should be labeled "Not for internal consumption." I'm what might be described as the "cheddar cheese" or "Einstein" of our family, while my older brother, Andy, might be labeled "cottage cheese—with extra lumps." In fact, some of the strange propensities displayed by Andy cause me to wonder if we are even related. Somebody here, and I am not saying who, must have been adopted.

Andy likes to canoe, fish, hike, and camp. He enjoys almost anything associated with the outdoors. In short, Andy likes to suffer. "Wait," you might say, "there are millions of people who enjoy those activities." You might be right. I can only hope those people receive their fair share of the agony due to them for their foolishness.

Unfortunately, they probably won't. Why not? Because

nature maintains an equilibrium in things such as temperature, moisture, suffering, and pain. Already, a large and disproportionate chunk of the agony dished out in the wilderness has been directed at Andy and anyone stupid enough to accompany him on one of his outings. These other people have probably even enjoyed themselves while on their adventures in the outdoors. Those of us with Andy have never been so lucky.

One of the more benign outdoor activities at which Andy became proficient was bird watching. At one time, he claimed he could identify any bird we pointed out to him. I took him up on the challenge on more than one occasion, and sure enough, he'd immediately rattle off the name of the bird. "That's a double-breasted, sap-sucking, bow-legged whippoorwill," he'd say, with a dangerously smug expression on his face. Dangerous because by appearing so smug, a calamity might befall him in the form of his brothers attempting to beat him to a pulp. He could do the same thing with snakes, always answering the pertinent question: Is it poisonous? Of course, I hardly knew the identities of any birds or snakes, except the crow, which I probably would confuse with a raven, so I blindly had to accept his answers. Once in a while, Andy did sort of back his answers up a little by betting with his life. At least to me, that's what it looked like he was doing.

I remember one time, and this was not an unusual case, as we scavenged beside the edge of a lake for whatever boys scavenge, Andy spotted a snake's head skimming along the surface of the water. My first thought was "Water Moccasin." As I said before, my thinking is rather one dimensional when it comes to birds and snakes. It's the same way most guys think about colors. There are just a few that I know. Birds come in black, blue, and red. Snakes are rattlers, garters, or moccasins. Actually, I can't really identify a moccasin, but if a snake's in the water, to me, it's a moccasin. Not to Andy.

Out he waded, about waist deep, to confront the sea

serpent. As Andy approached, the snake did an emergency dive right between his legs. Andy plunged his hands into the murky water and hauled the snake out. Yep, he was right, it wasn't poisonous. Maybe I should say that we'll never know if it was poisonous, because the snake didn't get a chance to bite Andy and prove otherwise.

Andy also seems to enjoy the cold. How can anyone in their right mind like being cold? Andy is sort of a cross between an Eskimo and a polar bear—completely immune to the cold and its effects. Once, in Virginia, we had a freak overnight storm that left a couple of feet of snow on the ground. Jumping at the chance to show off his knowledge of the outdoors, Andy put on his knickers. He wanted to demonstrate how warm and comfortable knickers are in the most extreme conditions. Confidently, he went tromping off into the snow with everything above the ankle and below the thigh exposed to the worst that Mother Nature had to offer. It felt like 20 below to me, but Andy was enjoying his romp in the snow. People for all these years had been fools, he proclaimed! You didn't need to actually cover up your skin during a blizzard. "Most of the heat leaves through your head," he said, as his knees turned blue, but he never complained.

No doubt about it, Andy proudly earns the title: "Cottage Cheese of the Family." However, his eccentricities have been useful to me at least a few times over the years. In fact, it's possible he's even saved my life once or twice, though usually from predicaments he tricked me into in the first place.

Once was on a camping trip in Pennsylvania in January. Stop. That should have been my first clue. January. What was I doing on a camping trip in January, complete with ice, wind, and snow? I was tricked, that's what. Now, of course, I wouldn't want to unjustly impugn anyone, so I'm not going to mention which older brother it was that was responsible for this trip.

The snow enveloped us in all the glistening beauty that

can only be found when it falls in heavy sheets in untouched wilderness. Gazing upon the quaint scene that would soon become our campground, I could only think of what a side of beef must feel like inside a meat locker; that's because I had already lost all feeling in my fingers and toes. As the sun receded behind the mountains, my hands went completely numb. We had yet to strike a match for a fire or drive a solitary stake in the ground for our tent. I stood there shivering, as useless as a tuxedo in a nudist colony.

Fortunately, Andy continued to function quite well and went about the task of digging up wood from beneath the snow, properly constructing a Boy Scout approved fire site, and finally starting a fire. I believe he said he started the fire by rubbing two sticks together, "just to see if it could be done —with wet wood in January." Never mind that I might have lost a couple of limbs to frostbite in the meantime.

Okay, I'm sure Andy did use a match on this occasion, but he is notorious for doing the strangest things "just to see if it can be done." Some of his challenges are harmless but weird: "Let's see who can balance on one foot the longest on top of this fence," or "Let's see how long we can juggle this Nerf ball with our feet while holding our breath and spinning a 360 after each pass." Others are not so benign: "Let's see who can hold this disgusting South American anti-Third World disease pill on his tongue the longest without swallowing," or "Let's see who can touch the fattest person" (this one was downright dangerous).

However, Andy did come through for me on that camping trip; otherwise I would have been a mid-winter frozen feast for bears, wolves, field mice, or whatever else they have in Pennsylvania. Another time he rescued me from certain demise was during a weeklong hiking (code for: Death March) and camping trip on the Appalachian Trail in the Shenandoah region of Virginia. Two close friends, Rick and Jeff, accompanied us. Jeff and I were in transition between the ninth and tenth grades. Andy and

Rick were between the tenth and eleventh.

I've concluded that a great deal of wisdom must be acquired in the tenth grade, because Andy and Rick had it all over Jeff and me, except for Rick's choice of shoes. We hiked more than 20 miles a day up and down steep mountain trails and the soles of Rick's Puma sneakers were so thin he might as well have gone barefoot. How he kept up, I'll never know. However, in every other aspect, Andy and Rick had us beat. They were more thorough, organized, knowledgeable about camping, and unafraid of meeting Bigfoot, the thought of which kept Jeff and me awake almost every night.

One sunny morning, Andy and Rick carefully packed their belongings. Probably three layers of garbage bags waterproofed each item. Jeff and I were tired of messing around with wasteful inconveniences such as waterproofing our packs, and seeing the day's clear sky, decided to expose our clothes and sleeping bags, allowing them to "air out" during the hike.

Approaching the summit of the highest mountain we would ascend on the entire trip, the temperature suddenly dropped and the heavens opened up. We were soaked to the bone. Soon, I began to shake uncontrollably. I became more useless than I had been on that January camping trip in the snow, if that were possible. How long it was before camp was set up and a fire was going? I don't know. I certainly had nothing to do with building either. However, as Andy and Rick worked feverishly on our site, Jeff and I did our part to halt the spread of hypothermia—to us. We quietly performed the ol' switch-a-roo with Andy's and Rick's sleeping bags. Having dry bags, one would think that Jeff and I slept soundly that night; unfortunately, as our older brethren drifted off into a sound slumber, we were wide awake, wondering, once again, if Bigfoot might pay us a visit before dawn. I should have known better than to be paired up with someone who would later in life view "E.T." as a horror flick.

On a more positive note, at least I didn't feel a twinge of guilt for having liberated Andy's dry bag to a more worthy cause. It never bothered me. Guilt is just one thing that can't exist in family relations. When it comes to dealing with my brothers, I've built up quite an immunity to guilt over the years. It's a good thing too; otherwise after all that's transpired between us, I'd probably have to be institutionalized today.

The third time Andy saved my life, he also can be credited with saving my daughters. We were in Idaho one summer, planning a pleasant day of floating down the Big Springs fork of the Snake River. This was the same trip Andy, our brother Brian, and I had taken the previous year. When my brothers and I navigated the frigid waters flowing from Big Springs, our main concerns consisted of:

1. Not getting a sunburn
2. Not being bitten by mosquitoes
3. Coming up with the next degrading remark about Brian's obvious lack of angling skills

Not to say that Brian was one of the worst fishermen ever to set foot in Idaho, but he should probably stick to tossing dynamite into a stock pond.

The trip looked as though it would be a mirror image of last year's. The sun was bright, and in case of emergency, each of us had a customized swarm of mosquitoes we could use as a form-fitting blanket. Originally, I planned on being the captain on this luxury cruise in our three-man rubber raft with just the "saboteurs"—also known in some parts as my daughters, Rachel (10) and Robyn (7)—along as the crew. Having learned from harrowing experiences in the past, I prepared to depart on the trip with plenty of junk food. No jackets or waterproof bags to keep our clothing dry were necessary, but we packed plenty of food. A person can get mighty hungry floating down a river for four hours.

Providence intervened, and Andy decided to join us. He filled up precious space in our raft with two coats, a poncho, and a custom-fitted Australian Bush hat, amongst other worthless, non-edible items. We also had another mouth to feed, and a big one at that. Our preparations complete, off we went.

What started out as a perfect day abruptly deteriorated into a chilling nightmare as a storm rolled in over the mountains. We were just shy of fifty minutes into our day-long float trip when the temperature plummeted. Then, I heard a sound that I thought belonged to an inconsiderate speedboat on its way to ruin our little piece of paradise. Turning to look up the river, I saw a wall of hail cutting into the water like the blades of a reaper. The impact was horrific. The girls screamed in pain. I felt the sting of the hail despite wearing one of Andy's coats and the Aussie hat he'd allowed me to borrow. The wind blew furiously. Efforts to propel the raft with our kayak-style, two-bladed paddle were completely neutralized. In fact, the velocity of the wind was so great that it lodged us against the reeds that surrounded the entire river. There were no banks, just frigid, swamp-like waters for nearly half a mile in all directions. Later we would learn that two men canoeing nearby on Lake Yellowstone died the previous day in a similar sudden storm. For us, the ordeal had just begun.

As it filled with hail, the boat was rapidly becoming a deadly ice chest. With our movement paralyzed by the wind and the hail falling at even greater intensities, I realized it was time for a true, hardened outdoorsman to intervene and take command. Qualified, since I'd spent a couple of days at the family log cabin that summer, I took charge. My first order demonstrated that I had a complete grasp of the situation. "We'll just sit here and wait the storm out," I bellowed. Andy, probably scared senseless due to the girls' screams, the sting of hail, and a new arrival on the scene, lightning strikes, said, "We need to get out of the water, now!"

Saved again by divine intervention, we were blown into a cove that contained an island of actual dry land. In that torrent of wind and hail, this was the only land we could have reached with our rubber raft. Here, I made an indisputably heroic contribution to the trip. I paddled with such ferocity that the metal staff of our paddle was bent by the time we reached the island's bank.

Andy pulled the boat ashore. I took Robyn in my arms. Knowing exactly what to do in such situations, I ran frantically around the little island. Robyn contributed to my stamina in this race to nowhere when she declared, "I'm going to die here!" Calmly, Andy announced, "We can't get under any trees, we'll use the raft for cover." To us, our little wigwam set up over a damp, decaying, old log, rivaled a room in the poshest hotel when compared to our circumstances on the river just a few minutes before.

About an hour later, the storm lost some of its intensity and we decided to head back to the river. Andy asked me to separate our one paddle into two so that both of us would have one. Remembering that I had bent one end of the paddle, I decided to press it against the ground in order to straighten it out; it snapped like a twig. My genius had now relegated us to a single paddle and I wasn't through "helping" yet. We placed the boat back into the water and climbed aboard. Using my uncanny sense of direction, I immediately began paddling our craft toward safety. Andy started to protest. Obviously confused, he yelled, "You're going the wrong way!" Siding with Andy, Rachel and Robyn joined the fray. Our ordeal must have taken its toll on my unfortunate shipmates. All of them had become hopelessly disoriented. Still, I reconsidered. There was at least a slim chance that those three were correct and I might be a tad mistaken. They must have made a lucky guess, because as it turned out, I *was* going the wrong way.

After we found our way back to the river, Andy insisted on taking over the paddling job; it was not that he was displeased with my efforts, he just wanted to get some feeling back in his left arm, which had gone numb during the storm. Unfortunately, his arm refused to work. Something had induced paralysis in his arm, a condition that would be with him for about two weeks. Under normal circumstances, his paralysis would have provided an excellent opportunity to dish out some brotherly abuse, but I was forced to defer. The hail was still with us, and we were far from safety.

Finally, we encountered a cabin along the river. The kindhearted owners took us in, let us dry up, and treated the girls to hot chocolate. They also gave Andy a lift into town, but not before he made his best effort to convince us to let him run back, just to see if it could be done frozen, half-dead, and with a paralyzed arm. He returned with his wife, Stephanie, their baby, Chandler, and our warm, dry car.

Proving that matches really are made in heaven, Stephanie said she felt as though she had "missed out" by not being with us on the raft during our adventure. All I have to say to Stephanie is, if it will make you happy, I'll be glad to fill up a bathtub with ice and let you sit in it. Of course, to complete the effect, we'll have to turn the shower on fully cold, bring in a huge fan, and play "hot potato" with a hair dryer.

I don't know how things would have turned out if Andy had decided not to go with us. Of course, I would have employed all of the many survival techniques I have acquired over the years, meaning that at least our bodies would have turned up within a week. I suppose I'm just thankful I never had the opportunity to find out what would have happened on the river that day without him. It is possible that some types of cottage cheese do have a purpose in this life.

The Dress

Recently, I have felt compelled to confess some of the slight infractions I committed against my younger brother Brian during our childhood. A possible explanation for the timing of this confession might be that over the years, I have matured and realized the importance of confessing transgressions against my fellow man, even if that fellow man is my younger brother. Ha! Not likely. The only reason I dare bring up this sordid subject now is that the tide of events has shifted in my favor.

First of all, I'm counting on Brian to have "matured" sufficiently that he will be way too far out of condition to consider any physical retribution against me. In my opinion, he has indeed matured nicely. Secondly, I believe I have compiled sufficient evidence to demonstrate what a profoundly compassionate older brother I was. This evidence far outweighs any so-called wrongs I may have accidentally committed. The final and most compelling reason is that I have unearthed conclusive evidence that proves my parents caused far greater and more permanent damage to Brian than I ever could have. As is usually the case, the weight of research by the scientific community falls heavily in my favor.

We need look no further than the respected field of psychology. Who always gets the blame for the behavior of arsonists, mass murderers, terrorists and fingernail biters? Parents, of course. Have you ever heard of a prominent murder trial where the defense lawyer points to the accused's older brother and says, "My client received irreparable brain damage from being forced to sniff his brother's smelly feet," or "My client is innocent, since he was psychologically damaged because his older brother used to hold him down and tickle him until he cried?" You will never hear defenses like these. The defense is far more likely to zero in on the gold mine of a negligent mother or father.

Lawyer for mass murderer: "I can PROVE that my client's parents didn't allow him to drive until he was sixteen."

or

"These people raised my client's allowance ONLY a paltry dollar, just once each year."

or

"My client was FORCED to eat his vegetables."

Certainly, it has been verified time and again in our courts of law that parents have had most damaging influence on each of us. My brother Brian's experience is no exception. Don't think for a minute that I've excluded myself as a victim, either. However, let us use this time for shedding light on the injuries and anguish suffered by my innocent brother.

Although, it is worth mentioning the time I was in a hardware store shopping with my mother. She lost sight of me for all of two seconds, and began to call out my name so loudly that everyone in the store must have thought I had something to do with a blue light special. To avoid a teenager's most feared demise, death by humiliation, I had no choice but to go into hiding behind a large display of paint cans. Unfortunately, my embarrassment was complete when my mother zeroed in on me and dragged me out of my sanctuary for all to see. How deeply was I scarred from this callous incident? Only time will tell. A total breakdown can occur years after being victimized by a parent. Fortunately, my parental-induced traumas were generally short in duration; this was not so for my brother Brian. With a single parental faux pas, Brian was to be traumatized for weeks, or more precisely, for an entire basketball season.

Brian and I were on the same basketball team. He was in the fourth grade and I was in the seventh. This season would be the only time in our lives that we would play on the same sports team together. It's too bad, too; it was rather entertaining to have Brian on my team. I'm sure we would have made one of sport's histories great brother duos, like, well, I can't think of any, but surely we would have been one of them, if it weren't for what happened to Brian even before the first tip-off.

Because of the age differences on our team, we had quite a disparity in the sizes of the players. Brian was the smallest, at barely 60 pounds, and the largest was my best friend, Roger, who topped out at about 190. Nike hadn't yet discovered our team, the Hawks, so we lacked funding for basically everything. Our team's colors were black and black (both the jersey and the shorts) and we had to take what clothing was given to us by the league.

This sort of potluck meant we were getting shirts and shorts that had been passed down for eons by prior generations of aspiring basketball players. You could only hope the jersey you received had been at least mildly detoxified with soap and water before it was issued to you.

"Issued" is a rather strong word to use for the free-for-all we had while struggling to get the jersey number and size we wanted. Actually, it wasn't exactly a free-for-all, either; there was a distinct pecking order in the distribution of our team's uniforms—age and ability before shrimps. Being at the top of the food chain, I selected my preferred jersey number and acquired a pair of perfect fitting shorts. Roger didn't have much competition in claiming a set that would cover his beefy frame. However, the selection in his size of XXXL was limited.

Finally, bringing up the rear, Brian poured over the tattered remains of available uniforms. Not much was left to choose from in the basket of moth-eaten jerseys. Quickly, he grabbed a shirt that would be baggy, no doubt, but would still do the job. Next it was over to the bin of basketball shorts. Brian stepped up to gaze at what had been left for him. It turned out that his choice was to be an easy one. Covering the bottom of the box was the only remaining pair of shorts. Brian reached in and retrieved what appeared to be a small and unusual looking black tent. A panicked second look revealed the box to be barren. There would be no choices for Brian. He was the proud new owner of the only other pair of shorts that would fit Roger, albeit loosely.

It wasn't quite as bad as it seems. Brian would, eventually, grow into these shorts—in about 22 years. However, at the present time, he faced the daunting task of keeping them pulled up and on. He also had to keep them under control, because when slipped onto his body, these shorts seemed to take on a life of their own, swelling out like a flower in full bloom.

Brian already sported extremely skinny legs (an anatomical configuration I occasionally reminded him of about 20 or 30 times a day), but these shorts made those legs look like white toothpicks protruding from a charred, jumbo marshmallow. It can only be imagined what went through Brian's mind the first time he considered actually displaying his body in these shorts on the basketball court in front of a live audience who would gaze at him for 48 minutes during each game. Some of these people knew him by name. Some even went to his school.

I can tell you this, there exists no force in nature powerful enough to have coerced me into even trying on a pair of shorts like those, let alone prancing up and down a basketball court in them. Just the same, there is not the slightest possibility I would ever expect (or allow) one of MY children to humiliate themselves, and more importantly, me, by being seen in such a monstrosity.

To his credit, Brian really didn't want to be a transvestite every Saturday morning. Also, he wasn't the only family member to have trouble with basketball and clothing. Our cousin Todd must have inherited this same gene. Running late for warm-ups before his high school basketball game, Todd raced out of his team's locker room. The crowd was already seated in the bleachers. Todd pulled off his sweats and sprinted to the other side of the court, putting in a perfect layup. Perfect, except that all he was wearing was a jock strap. Out of the far door he fled, not to be seen again for the rest of the evening.

Todd's embarrassment was unintentional—I think. So what compelled Brian to degrade himself each weekend in front of a live audience? Perhaps, he was convinced that our parents were always on the verge of bankruptcy. Therefore, they could not afford the five bucks for the pair of shorts necessary to preserve his dignity. In retrospect, I would have to agree with Brian on that one. Five dollars was probably a tad too steep price to pay for his self-respect. Do you have any idea how many candy bars you could get for five bucks back in 1975?

So, every Saturday our team would show up on the basketball court, most of us ready to play ball. However, Brian had one thing on his mind—the final buzzer that would end his weekly degradation. In the meantime, as the teams sprinted up and down the court, Brian—and you have to picture this—Brian would stand on the court, cross his legs, and use his hands to roll up the prodigious amount of excess gym short on each side in a vain attempt to achieve normalcy.

Of course, this unique pose detracted from his ability to have even a statistical impact on the game. Having his arms pinned to his sides may have lessened, at least slightly, his ability to register in such categories as:

Shots made – 0
Shots attempted – 0
Assists – 0
Passes caught – 0
Rebounds – 0

If the game were soccer, he may have fared at least a little better, in that you don't need your arms for soccer. In basketball, not having arms was a definite handicap. In all honesty, there were times Brian did manage to release his pants, which allowed his game to…bloom. Unfortunately, even in full bloom, his game was more akin to weeds than roses. Brian was still way too self-conscious to be bothered by such trivial matters as actually catching passes and grabbing rebounds.

Sickened by the entire affair, at last there arose an opportunity for me to help my brother where my parents had failed. I was going to miss one of our games while I was on a Boy Scout camping trip. Lacking any sense of decency, Brian, inquired as to whether he could use MY shorts for the game that weekend. Naturally, I would have loved to allow my brother to borrow my shorts, thereby restoring his pride and self-respect, but I declined his request for perfectly valid reasons that I can't remember at this particular time. I'm certain that my rationale on the matter was sane, reasonable, and practical. Therefore, I was surprised when my mother intervened and insisted that Brian be allowed to use them. With my father looming in the background, cheerfully...I acquiesced.

Now that it is years down the road, and Brian and I have sort of reached adulthood, the family can just sit around and laugh lightheartedly together about embarrassing memories like this one. Right? Ha! Wrong-O. My parents still feel the sting of wrath from Brian whenever someone, and I won't say who, dredges up the memory of the basketball shorts. I feel so horrible about what happened to him that as soon as I can catch my breath from laughing, I'm going to sit down and write that confession I promised.

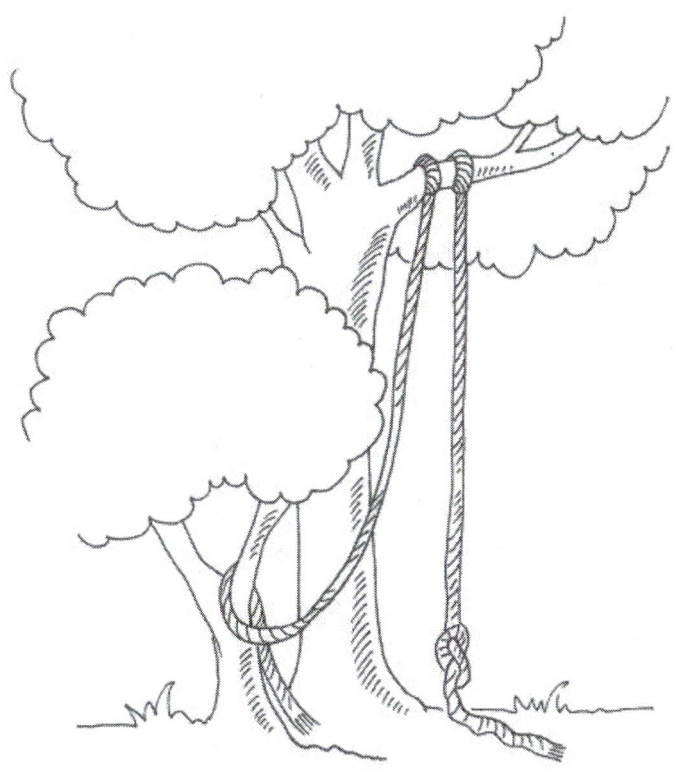

Working Out

I'm obsessed, addicted—label me with whatever degrading terms you couch potatoes use to describe those of us who enjoy the simple pleasure of seeing our toes whenever we're standing. Of course, it is only through a strict regime of diet and exercise that makes it possible to enjoy playing "this little piggy" without the assistance of a chiropractor. Since my diet is strict, that is, strictly ice cream and chocolate, I'm required to place substantial weight on the "exercise" portion of the fitness equation.

I suppose there is a certain amount of sickness involved with any individual who has an unquenchable urge to punish himself with an extreme exercise routine every other day or so. I don't know what happened to me. I started off as an almost normal kid, grew up in a nearly normal family, and evolved into a relatively normal adult. So what happened? I believe it all started when my father introduced me to the sport of wrestling at the age of nine.

Before my formal introduction to the sport, I thought I already knew all there was to know about wrestling. It went something like this: First, you tackle someone (preferably a little brother). Then, you hold him down. Finally, you tickle him, punch him, or make him eat dirt, depending on which particular crime the offending party is guilty. Usually, just being a younger brother served as a sufficient infraction to warrant one or more of the punishments listed above.

Actually, my younger brother Brian is one of the primary reasons for my relatively bizarre condition today. I probably would never have started wrestling and working out if it weren't for Brian. Not that he encouraged me. He hadn't the faintest idea that he was the reason I entered wrestling. My decision was a simple one, based on the lowest level of Maslow's Hierarchy of Needs—survival. I thought it was imperative to my self-preservation to not allow Brian to learn wrestling if I didn't know it myself. Believe me; I didn't want to go through the hard work of acquiring wrestling skills. I simply had no choice, since Brian might learn the moves and use them, unfairly, against me. I had no doubt he'd be able to do it, too.

My dad introduced Brian and me to wrestling by taking us to a demonstration. It just so happened that the two demonstrators were both about my size and age. I was in awe of their skills. More to the point, I was mortified when I saw the moves they performed. There was no way I was going to join that team, go to practice, and have these two pint-sized Arnold Schwarzeneggers beat me to a pulp. As far as I was concerned, my wrestling career was over.

Enter my dumb brother, Brian, who had none of my misgivings. He intended to go forward with the plan. I was flabbergasted by his foolishness. Did he want to be thrown down on his back, have his face rubbed in the mat by these Neanderthals, and be humiliated? Was he nuts? Then again, whatever happened to him at wrestling practice couldn't be any worse than the tortures he had to endure on a daily basis at my hands. After pondering his decision for a moment, I felt a spike of fear shoot through me. If Brian were to learn this wrestling stuff, he'd be able to take ME down. He'd be able to twist MY arms behind my back. He'd be able to mash MY face in the dirt. These were my God-given rights—the rights of an older brother. Brian wasn't in the club. I wasn't about to sell him my birthright either, and in good conscience, I couldn't allow him to upset the delicate balance of nature.

What had looked like a choice was no choice at all. I could either be humiliated at the hands of strangers, or humiliated at the hands of my younger brother. I was at practice the next week.

Surprisingly, I found that I was fairly natural at the sport. Those two guys in the demo were easy pickings for me after I learned just a couple of moves. In fact, all I had were two moves: the doubleleg takedown and a half-nelson. For that first year, those moves were all that I needed to go undefeated. Undefeated, that is, until we entered an "open" tournament.

Because of my record of all wins and no losses, I was the number one seed. I was paired up with some poor sap that had a losing record for the year. "Chump change," I thought. Unbeknownst to me, this guy was on a "traveling" team. That's a team that's so good they travel around looking for guys that can beat them. All I can remember about the match was spending the entire time on my back, which is not good in wrestling. He finally "pinned" me in the last period. I had given up, exhausted, from what seemed like a never-ending struggle. However, I swore I would never give up again, and I never did, although I was pinned once more in my life, but that's another story.

This desire to wrestle for survival turned into an obsession to win, and one way to win in wrestling was to be stronger and in better condition than your opponent. These facts fueled my need for extreme workouts. I found Brian to be superb at formulating ideas about working out—ideas for others to do. The pattern is recognizable. He thinks up the bizarre exercise that we will do and I end up being the only one to actually do it. In addition to his own grotesque way of inflicting pain during weight training, a couple of his ideas were pushing a car up and down hills in a parking lot and climbing a rope in my backyard. Brian concocted these ideas during my thirties, when my wrestling career was reincarnated. I decided to enter "open" wrestling tournaments against college, post-college, and in one case, Olympic-caliber wrestlers.

Brian knew that while I was at the Air Force Academy I used to sneak off and climb a rope that was used as part of the obstacle course. I would occasionally tell him what a fabulous workout that had been. One day, a few years ago, he decided that rope climbing would be the perfect way for "us" to get in shape. Looking at my backyard, he spied a large oak tree. About forty feet up was a fork in its trunk. "We'll tie it up there," Brian declared. *We*. I've always been fond of his use of the word "we." Last time I checked, that word always means more than one. However, somehow it happened that only one of us would actually undertake the task he had in mind. Somehow that someone never failed to be me. "We" would go jogging, only he would use a bike. "We" would indulge in his extreme weight training program, but he couldn't afford to get sore, so most of the lifting was left to me. Now, "we" were going to attempt to attach a rope forty feet up this oak tree.

The plan, as it fell together, was to have two ropes, the main climbing rope and a safety rope. For the climbing rope, Brian acquired the thickest rope he could find at a local marina. It was identical in girth to the ones I used to climb at the Academy. The safety rope was a nylon mountain climbing rope, complete with a harness and carabineers.

The purpose of this contraption, Brian explained, was to protect the person who was slugging his way up the climbing rope. The climber would step into the harness, the fit of which was similar to a baby's swing. The legs go in, but the climber is only supported up to his behind. Giving the climber protection all the way up, the support rope would be attached at the top to the fork in the tree. If the climber got tired and couldn't hold on, he was protected from going splat on the ground below by the safety rope being held by the spotter.

Standing about 25 feet up atop an extension ladder, I heaved the weighted end of the climbing rope over the fork in the tree. Now all that remained to secure the rope was to tie a slipknot that would slide up the rope all the way to the supporting branch. The difficulty laid with the reluctance of a rope that size to cooperate and "slip" to the top. To encourage the knot to slip into place, I deduced that one of us would have to take the free end of the rope and jump off the top of the ladder. Naturally, to ensure the most expedient results in securing the rope, the more massive of the two project engineers would be the logical choice to perform the necessary leap from the ladder. It was simple physics. However, Brian thought the plan to be of such brilliance that the honors and accompanying broken bones should be reserved entirely for the one who formulated the plan.

I survived that first jump and the many others it took to coax the slipknot to the top of the rope. Securing the safety rope was a more harrowing experience. It was held on the limb by a strap, which I (again) had to secure to the tree. I don't think our operation would be OSHA approved, but it worked. Our climbing contraption was finally ready.

"We" were going to get in great shape. Imagine the arms we would develop, climbing this rope day after day to the point of exhaustion, secure in the knowledge of being supported by one's own trustworthy brother. I, in fact, did use the rope extensively, sometimes with leg weights. It was great training for my posthumous wrestling career. I didn't have much use for the safety rope; the thought of falling 40 feet to the ground was a sufficient motivation to keep my hands firmly attached to the rope.

The safety rope remained primarily for Brian's use. We tied it around a fork in a neighboring tree for storage when Brian wasn't using it, which, as usual, was most of the time. I don't mean to imply that Brian didn't get his money's worth out of this project, but I will say that on one of his rare visits when he actually decided to climb the rope, he couldn't. The reason? When we went to untie the support rope, we found that it was now part of the tree. That's right. The tree had grown over and above the rope. The rope itself was now ensconced within the fork of the tree. Not exactly a mark of frequent use.

That is, I found, an inconvenience about trees. They are always growing. In my opinion, a tree once trimmed should always remain that way, but our climbing tree continued to grow. Branches lined the path to the top of rope and they began to encroach on my climbing space. At first I would just climb around the branches, which would slap at my face and arms as I ascended the rope.

Unfortunately, as the weather became warmer, the branches brought with them an assortment of bugs and spiders. This situation was something altogether different. I would be completely exhausted, trying to focus on just putting one hand over the other. Then, nearing the apex of the climb, I'd spy some gigantic spider dangling directly in my path. After a few such intimate encounters, I concluded it was time to trim the branches back. I knew I would need

Brian's help. I also knew he'd be worthless at performing any of the actual climbing and cutting.

We decided to exploit our own natural strengths and talents to accomplish the task. I would climb and cut, while Brian would act as the anchor. The plan was for me to don the harness, attach the electric trimmer to my belt with the cord in tow, climb to the top of the rope, and start trimming. Once at the top, I would just hang there while Brian held me in place using the safety rope we recently had cut free from the grasp of the carnivorous tree trunk. Brian's task was to lower me to the next section after I finished cutting all the branches within my reach.

Preparing to climb, it occurred to me how tired I already was from doing my rope climbing earlier in the day. Also, the rope was slick and the ground muddy from some heavy rains that had passed through. I decided that all these minor inconveniences would just add to the workout. Up the rope I went. Brian supported me by wrapping the rope around his ample backside and walking backward, away from the tree, taking the slack as I went up.

Nearing the top, the trimmer broke free from my belt and spiraled down into the mud. Wearily, I told Brian to slacken the rope so I could climb back down and retrieve the tool. It was then that a terrible thought flashed through my mind, "If Brian doesn't lower me, I could be suspended, endlessly, up here in this harness. I'm at Brian's mercy." One of my rules in life is, "Never put yourself at your brother's mercy. He has none." Surely he wouldn't do that? Would he? With so much strenuous work ahead of me those thoughts vanished as quickly as they came.

We retrieved the fallen trimmer and reattached it securely to my belt. Back up the rope I went, biceps groaning all the way. All branches within reach were cut down to nubs. Then, Brian lowered me a little to the next group. Grasping the rope with one hand and trimming with the other, my strength was sapped even further.

Bit by bit, the tree was cut back to suitable rope climbing proportions. At last, I neared the end. I was suspended only about six feet off the ground and was making my final assault on the renegade branches, when I looked over at Brian. He had moved behind a smaller tree and was wrapping some of the safety rope around it. I didn't like the looks of things, but I didn't dare let Brian know I didn't like the looks of things.

As nonchalantly as possible, I inquired, "What's going on down there?"

Brian suspiciously responded, "Just tying some of this rope off." I reasoned this might be a prime time to get out of the support harness, but there was only one way to do it: climb. I had to climb high enough to get slack in Brian's rope so I could slither out of the harness.

With every muscle in my arms throbbing, I reached high on the rope and began a slow ascent. I knew I might not have much time. Slack had just begun to develop in the safety rope when Brian looked up. "What are you doing!?" he queried.

"Nothing," I said, "Some of these branches up here need a little more trimming." Lying has just never been one of my stronger suits, but I thought this one would probably fool Brian. He wasn't fooled in the least.

"Oh, no you don't!" he yelled, as he sprinted toward me from behind the tree. Brian had no intention of allowing his helpless victim to escape. I had gained just enough slack in the rope to begin wiggling out of the harness. Not fast enough. Brian was nearly on me. Desperately, I flipped upside down, hoping to fall out of the harness. As an old Chinese proverb reminds us, "It is better to land on one's head than be helplessly abused by younger brother."

One leg was free. I was almost out. One down, one to go. Stuck. I couldn't believe it. My left foot was tangled in the harness. As I swung upside down, suspended by one foot, Brian laughed a devilishly evil laugh. I should have deciphered his plot long before I got into this mess. He intended to secure the rope, leave me hanging about five feet off the ground, and apply a variety of nefarious tortures to both my body and my mind.

My efforts had only aided his cause. This was even better than his twisted mind had conceived. I was dangling like a spider at the end of a thread. As Brian laughed at me, he sent me spinning helplessly around. He cackled with delight as my head went deep into the mud. I had to think fast or else suffer what would undoubtedly be even greater indignities at my brother's hand.

It's important at this point to make note of the fact that, had the roles been reversed, I would never have stooped to so low a level as to take advantage of one of my brothers in like manner—another one of the injustices of life. It is at times like these that I am comforted by the knowledge that "the meek shall inherit the Earth." In this confrontation with Brian, I had a head start. I had already "inherited," meekly of course, a good deal of the Earth through my ears, nose, and mouth.

Suddenly, fortune smiled my way. My obviously vulnerable position carried with it a serendipitous manner of self-defense. Hanging upside down by one foot had the unforeseen advantage of placing my hands in a striking position against the feet of any attackers, namely, Brian. As he approached, I was able to reach out and grab his feet. He was more than slightly surprised to find himself tripping and falling onto our muddy battlefield.

As a veteran of many such wars, I was acutely aware of my opponent's ability to adapt to the changing conditions of our conflict. Any advantage I had achieved would be short lived. I had to act fast. That meant wiggling, and lots of it. Concentrating all my efforts on squirming and wiggling, I managed to free my trapped foot.

Free at last, I could now face my attacker on equal terms. As with most ignoble aggressors throughout history, Brian had no stomach for continuing the match on a level playing field; the contest ended in a draw. However, I felt a certain satisfaction in having wiled my way out of Brian's treacherous trap.

Dumber and Dumbest

I've written about my brother Andy's twisted love of the outdoors. Twisted may not be the right word; sadistic is probably more correct. Most normal people, when faced with exposure to the elements, attempt to shield themselves from it. I do that myself, by closing the front door; that's close enough to the elements for me. On the other hand, Andy always seems to seek out misery. He enjoys organizing canoeing, camping, fishing, and hiking trips, but always with an artistic bent.

For instance, one canoeing trip he dreamed up turned out to not include water. Check with any rafting or canoeing guide, and I guarantee they'll promise you that their trips involve water, but not Andy's. Rather than sitting in the canoe and floating down the "river" Andy chose, my father, brothers, and I were tasked with carrying the canoe over and under various obstacles in what appeared to be a trench. To Andy's credit, the trench did look as though someone had, at some time, inadvertently spilled some actual water into it. As we stumbled and tripped over the rocks, Andy kept reassuring us, "If there had been more rain, we wouldn't have to carry this canoe." I thought he might have said more "brain"—if we'd had more "brain." In that case, I would have to agree with him. If I had used mine, I would have passed on canoeing with Andy altogether.

However, one benefit of the trip was that my father was able to demonstrate his prowess in the martial arts. My brothers and I didn't even know he had taken karate lessons, but there he stood, having broken one of our useless paddles completely in two, using only his head. He claimed that he had slipped on a rock and his head had involuntarily struck the paddle as he fell into the canoe. However, I wasn't fooled by the cross-eyed expression on his face or the colorful welt growing across his forehead; I knew he was just showing off. Perhaps this was his way of warning my brothers and me not to even think of challenging his position of authority in the family. It was a drastic, but effective method he devised to make his point.

I was fortunate on many occasions NOT to accompany Andy on some of his harebrained adventures. Once without the unnecessary luxury of a tent, he and a friend went camping in the snow. "These sleeping bags are all we'll need," Andy explained. After Andy thawed out a few days later, you would think he might have had a change of heart, but he was as persistent as ever. Another time, after Andy did a winter climb up Mount Rainier, he gave me the following instructions: "Don't tell Mom, but I almost died." True, Mom might have been a little annoyed if he had resembled a giant Popsicle when he was shipped home, but at least she wouldn't have to worry any longer about snakes being brought into the house.

On another trip, this one 19,340 feet up Mount Kilimanjaro, apparently Andy felt the guides had only taken his group to about 19,339 feet. Andy was sick with something like the flu even before the climb began, but by golly, he was going to go to the top. Upset with Andy's request to continue the ascent, the Kenyan guide raced up the mountain at a blistering pace. How foolish. This guide didn't know that Andy thrives on things like coldness, wetness, asphyxiation, stupidity, and pain. After a few minutes, the guide sat down in disgust and told Andy he could go on by himself, which he did—all the way to some slight protrusion in the ground that might have signified the summit of Kilimanjaro.

Lately, I've been wondering if New Line Cinema is ever going to pay my brother Andy royalties for stealing his life story. The movie they made, "Dumb and Dumber," is clearly based on Andy. Perhaps executives at New Line thought they were safe legally, since the title didn't include the word "Dumbest." Let us look briefly at this comparison in levels of stupidity...

During their drive to Aspen, Colorado in "Dumb and Dumber," Lloyd and Harry trade in their dog mobile for a moped. They do this in the winter, but at least they are dry and near civilization. Andy and his roommate, Joe, begin their adventure on the Kenai Peninsula in Alaska. Don't know where that is? If you can picture the North Pole, you'll be close enough.

Andy and Joe decide to go fishing in the ocean, which is fine, since theoretically, only the fish are supposed to get wet. But we're talking Dumber and Dumbest here. Joe, thinking—and I use this term loosely—a fish he hooked is getting away, dives into the ice-cold water. Andy reflexively falls in face first himself. Getting soaking wet in Alaska can be dangerous. It's time to get home. Unfortunately, the tide comes in and cuts off the exit route.

Slugging through the briny water, Andy and Joe finally make it to the other side. What to do now? How about jumping on a motorcycle and driving back in the middle of the night? Sure, why not. Of course, unlike Lloyd and Harry, Andy and Joe run out of gas.

They come to a halt near the only building for miles, a fish-packing plant. Begging and then buying as much gas as they can, Andy and Joe replenish their motorcycle, and half-frozen, head home to their...tent. That's right; Andy and Joe are living in a tent. By comparison, after Lloyd and Harry complete their ride to Aspen, they check into a five-star hotel. Now, look at this chart to summarize the differences:

Lloyd and Harry	vs	Andy and Joe
Aspen		Alaska
Dry		Soaked
Gas		No Gas
Five-Star Hotel		Tent

Nothing more needs to be said, but I will. New Line Cinema made millions by creating two imaginary imbeciles, imbeciles that follow a script, a script that can show them to be as stupid as the writers want to make them. That's the purpose of the entire movie. However, their characters still can't hold a candle to Andy and Joe in raw, unabashed stupidity. I think this February I'm going to advise Andy to strap on a set of roller blades and head for the New Line Cinema headquarters, located in Kangamuit, Greenland, to demand his fair share of the proceeds from "Dumb and Dumber." Of course, he would probably enjoy the trip.

It's quite obvious that I don't quite share my brother's intense love of the outdoors, in that I don't enjoy frostbite, bugs, and/or close encounters with large man-eating mammals, reptiles, and fish. However, I do relish a little competition, and there is a certain satisfaction that can be attained in beating an extremist at his own game. One day, I saw just such an opportunity.

We were on one of Dad's "let's drive 15 hours a day" family vacations, as we passed through Yellowstone National Park. It has been scientifically proven that spending 10 or more hours in the backseat of a car, sandwiched between two hostile brothers, will drive any boy crazy. Confirming this theory, Andy announced another of his "brilliant" ideas. As he gazed at the steep, snow-covered mountainside stretching up to the sky, Andy concocted a plan. "Let's see who can run the furthest, barefoot, in the snow—up the mountain," he challenged.

Past experiences with Andy made me wary of this plan from the start. However, having always being the greater of two fools (that is, the fool that follows a fool), I began to think: *Andy is always known for being so tough in the outdoors. What if I actually beat him at his own game? I'd dethrone Andy as the family outdoorsman and tough guy.* As I contemplated the spoils that victory would bring, the reality of unavoidable suffering entered my mind. *But look*, I thought, *this is not a weeklong camping, hiking, body-destroying experience like he usually thinks up. I can run up this mountain, triumph over both of my brothers, and be in a warm, heated car all within a few minutes.*

My strategy began to unfold. First of all, there was no way I was going to endure the agony that awaited me without assured success. I had to win, period. Therefore, the only way I could ensure victory was to go last. After my brothers ran, I could ascertain the exact distance up the mountain that was required for victory.

Brian went first. He hopped and skipped a meager distance in the snow and quickly made a beeline for the sanctuary of the car. Next was Andy. I wasn't disappointed. He went perhaps 50 yards up the snow-covered mountain, sinking sometimes above his knees. Then, all of a sudden, Andy got a look of urgency on his face. In turbo-mode, he returned directly to the car, and I thought he was humbled a bit by the experience. He deserved it. After all, it was his idea. Now it was my turn, and I intended to leave no question as to whom the victor was. I took off—sans shoes—up the mountain as quickly as my skinny legs would carry me.

At first I thought, "This is easy!" I passed Brian's distance without a wince, and as I zoomed by Andy's mark, I shouted, "This is nothing!" I ascended the mountain 50 yards, 75 yards, and then, as I approached the point at which I would double Andy's distance, I began nonchalantly strolling up the mountain. My brothers stared at me in amazement. *Bet I can go to the top,* I thought. Suddenly, I sank chest deep in the snow. At that precise moment, the nerves in my feet sent a desperate signal, to my brain: "Get out, you fool!" Perceiving the situation in a split-second, I concurred that I needed to be out NOW. Having as far to go down as I had just gone up, I knew I was in trouble. I raced down the slope, sinking and stumbling with each step.

I am now able to answer a question that has mystified many wise men over the centuries, but only because they were too intelligent to find out the answer. That question is: "How does it feel to run barefooted for an eternity in deep snow?" Those of you who think your feet eventually go numb have obviously never run barefoot in the snow. The best description for the unique sensation each time a foot touches the snow is that of a dozen foot-long knives penetrating through the sole of the foot and then shooting straight up through the knee.

Victory and all its spoils were mine. Of course, during the run down, I didn't have any brain capacity available to think about all those spoils. Every last brain cell in my head (all 42 of them) was tasked with sending the message to my feet: "Run faster!" About three and half years later, I finally arrived at the car, capturing the title of "Grand Family Champion of the Elements." Not hardly. In fact, each one of us is more likely to receive a title more fitting of our performance in that competition:

Brian – "Dumb"
Andy – "Dumber"
Me – "Dumbest"

I wore that title with pride. After all, it's not easy to strip Andy of a title he held (and would hold again) without equal for so many years.

Cars

Recently, I had a liberating experience. I wrecked my new car. How is wrecking a car liberating? Well, the body shop and car rental company liberated me from a significant amount of my money. However, I'm certain my insurance company will be more understanding. They have assured me that I will be able to cover the expected premium increase by giving no more than three quarts of blood each week. Of course, under the new plan for "at-risk" drivers, a one-time donation of a kidney, spleen, or lung is required as prepayment. You can't help but admire the flexibility offered to the consumer by today's insurance companies.

So far, most of my cash has gone to the car rental company, as I had to wait three weeks for the return of my vehicle from the body shop. I'm sure there's a logical explanation for the lethargy demonstrated by the body shop in repairing my car. It could be that the proprietor of the rental car company is the body shop owner's half-brother, or maybe, the body shop guys know that if they snap one panel off and snap one back on in the five minutes it actually takes to do the job, they can't justify the $5,000 they're charging for making the repairs. It is much more lucrative for the body shop guys to play paper football in the break room for the first 20 days and then snap the panels back on during day 21, unless of course the football game runs into overtime. Overtime requires the car to remain in the shop for an extra week with the mechanics being paid time-and-a-half. Whatever the reason for the delay, I was required to become intimately familiar with my rental car.

I still treasure the memory of those weeks in September driving that 1927 model Ford Escort that came without the unnecessary luxuries of FM stereo, air conditioning, brakes, or steering. I considered it sort of a "back to nature" adventure, which is fortunate, because that makes me exempt from this year's "Hike and Camp 'Til You Drop" expedition sponsored by my brother Andy. I haven't worked on my excuse for next year, but if I'm lucky, I'll break a leg or drop into a coma before he calls. Anyway, forget the $5,000 repair cost, my three weeks of driving that Escort were my true penance for the accident. Fortunately, the agony that car put me through was not without some merit—I saved at least four dollars by not renting a current model.

In addition to providing me with a lesson in frugality, my accident also proved to be an enlightening experience in other ways. Don't think that I was elated to have wrecked my car, but the accident provided me with the opportunity I had been waiting for since I first stepped into the world of car ownership (gentility prevents me from saying what that is like stepping in). Now, I was empowered to try out my Theorems of Car Ownership. These theorems were developed over a painstakingly slow and expensive process of making nearly every wrong decision possible with the cars I owned in the past. The theorems are:

1. Never buy a used car

2. Never drive a car one mile or one minute—whichever comes first—past its warranty

3. Always have "collision insurance"

4. Always have "other than collision insurance"

5. Always have "other than whatever the other than collision insurance does not cover insurance"

Let's look at the sound scientific method used in developing each of these theorems. First, never buy a used car. This leaves only one option: Buy a new car. Stay with me on this. I know many people may say that they have bought or have friends who have bought used cars, driven them for years, and never had any problems. There is a simple explanation for this: They are lying. No one wants to admit they were snookered.

Buying a used car is like playing an expensive version of hot potato. The first owner waits to sell his car until he believes he's in danger of having the transmission explode into thousands of pieces on the interstate during rush hour. Of course, the transmission does explode, but if timed correctly, that memorable event happens to the sucker who bought the car from him. Believing he's seen the worst of the problems with his new dream machine, the second owner drives the car until he's dumped about half his life savings into it, and then he tries to unload it on some unlucky slob before the car REALLY starts to cost him big bucks. This process churns through several iterations of foolhardy owners, until *I* end up buying the car.

Admittedly, I did own a used car once that could be considered reliable, if starting and stopping it with a screwdriver doesn't disqualify it from that category. That car was a 1980 Datsun 210, and it did, in fact, require no keys to operate. My Datsun delivered the complete Japanese driving experience of that era, in the sense that you knew if you ever had a wreck in your 210, the flimsy aluminum hull would be crushed down to the dimensions of a single-serving sized can of dog food. This convenient collapsible car design meant your family's funeral expenses would be minimal, and the rescue crew could dispose of the whole mess in a paper bag; all provided to you by Datsun at no extra charge.

My Datsun did give me the advantage of never having to worry about locking my keys in the car, since they never left my pocket. However, one time I pulled into my squadron parking lot, jumped out of my car, and went on a mission of five or six hours piloting the USAF KC-10 Extender. Upon returning to my car at the completion of the flight, I noticed that something didn't look quite right. There was smoke coming out of my car's exhaust pipe; the car was running. In my haste to go off to defend the free world, I never bothered to use the screwdriver to shut off the engine. Lucky for me, the Datsun had a go-cart sized engine, so it hadn't run out of gas.

The first car I ever owned was also a used car, a red 1968 Camaro convertible. I acquired this mechanical marvel in Georgia during my three-week stint in what I considered, as an Air Force Academy cadet, the bowels of ignorance: U.S. Army Airborne Jump School. The reason I purchased that car was that I was sure women would like it. They did; they just didn't like seeing my shaved head behind the wheel, driving it. That car was beautiful to me for about one month and then I wrecked it on my drive back to the federal penitentiary, Colorado division, euphemistically known as the U.S. Air Force Academy. Additional Theorem of Car Ownership: Don't drive a car unless its tires have a visible tread. My Camaro's previous owner had bought the best tires he could find—for five dollars. The lapse in quality rubber on my vehicle was obvious, so I decided to replace the tires just as soon as I arrived at the Academy. I did exactly that, but not before I customized the left side of my car by sliding into an available guardrail for an artistic impression. That Camaro was destined to teach me almost all of the lessons I would need to learn about cars. From the knowledge I've acquired, I believe we'd all be better off if we joined the Amish.

After spending roughly 2,257 hours underneath that car, I should be an ASE-certified mechanic. Unfortunately, I don't remember much from all of my labors, and the majority of the problems with my car could not be fixed, at least not with any of the tools I had on hand. Yet another Theorem of Car Ownership: Don't bother buying any tools. No matter how many tools you buy, you will never ever have the one you need to repair your car. In any case, no tools could have helped me. Big bucks were needed to replace *entire* sections of that Camaro, and my $100-200 a month paycheck would not allow me that luxury. My lack of resources made life simple. I pretty much just had to live with my car's cosmetic shortcomings the way they were.

How aesthetically challenged was my Camaro? Obviously, I couldn't afford to repair the damage done by the guardrail; however, I found ways to use that new look to my advantage, I was King of the Road, in that people always got out of my way when I pulled up behind them. You'd think they were afraid that I didn't know how to drive or something—as if *they* had never had a little fender bender during their lifetimes. The Camaro also sported a large crack that went all the way across its windshield. Sure, that crack cut back on the visibility a little, but with the top down I could always look *over* the windshield. I love convertibles.

My Camaro wasn't the best passenger vehicle either, especially if the passengers were wearing nice clothes (nice defined as: anything other than pre-stained mechanic's jeans). The upholstery was supposed to be white, but it was a genuine rust color that was enhanced each time a passenger folded one of the seats forward. As the seat went forward, large quantities of rust came pouring out of the seatback. That's how I knew the upholstery's tint was the real McCoy.

The Camaro came equipped with a couple of distinctive standard features. For one, it had a primitive cruise control system. To the best of my knowledge, cruise control was unavailable in 1968, but my Camaro had it. The cruise control system was simple and fully automatic. When the gas pedal was pressed down, it stayed right where it was. No fancy wires and buttons were needed. Of course, stopping was a bit tricky, but it took only a few weeks to get used to driving the car with my foot *under* the gas pedal.

My Camaro also came with an automatic oil changing system, a feature still not available on new cars purchased today. All I had to do was drive the car as far as half of a tank would take me (about 50 miles) and voila, miraculously, one quart of oil would be removed from the crankcase. I just had to remember to add another quart of oil every time I shut the engine off or at every stop light, whichever came first.

Another innovative feature of my Camaro was its powerful air conditioning system. The only drawbacks were that it cooled only in the winter, and it only had one setting: full cold. I believe the key to this ingenious system was in blocking up the entire engine cooling system with free-floating rust. It was easy to recognize me when I was driving down a Colorado road in the middle of winter (temperature −20F). I was the frozen blue object in the red Camaro whose engine was engulfed in steam from overheating.

However, what endeared me the most to that first car was how the Camaro assisted me in learning the basics of behavioral psychology. It was mandatory to take Psychology 101 at the Academy, and here I was, blessed with an off-campus laboratory on wheels. My Camaro's specialty was in "Testing the Effects of Negative Reinforcement on Driver Behavior while Simultaneously requiring the Driver to apply Maslow's Hierarchy of Needs."

The required materials for my off-campus study program were my windshield wiper controls, some form of precipitation and one slightly neurotic driver. As with most items on the Camaro, my windshield wiper system was partly defective. It worked fine for the first five or ten minutes after I purchased the car. Subsequently, I became the subject of a behavioral experiment with the dashboard mounted wiper button serving as the instrument of antagonism.

Experiment Phase I: Wipers quit functioning with the switch in the "On" position

Quickly adapting to the change in my environment, I discovered that the wipers would work, but only if the wiper button was pressed—one press, one wipe. This system worked respectably in light rain. Once again, my Camaro was ahead of its time. I had intermittent wipers. I merely waited until the moisture built up sufficiently on the windshield to the point where my vision was so obscured that I could hardly see anything smaller than a semi coming head-on, and then I pressed the button. For that simple action, I was rewarded with one swish of the blades and the ability to see without sticking my head out of the window; better than a lump of cheese at the end of a maze.

Experiment Phase II: Increased precipitation

Things became a bit more risky when the rain began to fall with increasing intensity. Aware of the fact that it was sometimes necessary to see out of the windshield to drive my car, I would frantically operate the wiper button with my left hand while driving with my right. Had my car been stick shift, only an octopus would have been capable of driving it under adverse weather conditions. One arm to press down on the gas pedal, one to pull the gas pedal back up, one for steering, one for the stick shift, one for pressing the wiper button, and a spare arm for senseless tasks I've never found necessary, such as operating the turn signals. Of course, this is pure fantasy. An invertebrate would never be found driving one of my cars, because invertebrates aren't that stupid. I, on the other hand, had advanced to Phase III of the experiment.

Experiment Phase III – Shock treatment

Phase III began in a benign enough fashion. If I desired the privilege of driving *and* seeing out the windshield at the same time, I would receive a mild electric shock through the wiper button each time it was pressed. In Phase II, all that was required of me was to press the wiper button whenever I wished; however, in Phase III, I had to determine if it were really necessary to remove the two inches of snow on my windshield to drive. If I arrived at that self-serving conclusion, I would be rewarded with a jolt of electricity. Gradually, the voltage began to increase until it reached a level that should be reserved exclusively for persons convicted on first-degree murder charges. As the voltage increased, I progressed from driving while gritting my teeth to wearing thick, insulated gloves. Nothing worked. The electricity was penetrating whatever I wore for protection. I was beginning to feel like the main course for Meals on Wheels. As usual, my Camaro had proved that it was ahead of its time. I was driving the first production electric car.

Before my hair became bleached white, I decided it was time to pass my noble driving machine on to a more deserving motorist. I found selling my car to be a rather troublesome ordeal. The trouble wasn't that the Camaro had almost every mechanical problem known to mankind. The trouble was that I couldn't bring myself to lie about any of it. After weeks of rejection, I was finally rewarded with the car salesman's dream: a dad with a son who "just had to have" my car.

I don't want to misrepresent my part in this sale. When this pair of prospective buyers approached me, I didn't blurt out, "This is a '68 Camaro that contains more rust than iron, you can see over the windshield, but not through it, almost as much oil as gas is required to operate it, only drive it in the winter if you don't find the effects of frostbite uncomfortable, and make certain your life insurance policy is current if you decide to use the wipers." No, no, my intention was to inform, not to discourage. So, when posed with the questions like, "Does it burn oil?" I would look pensive for a moment and reply slowly, "Well, yes it does, and you know the thing about burning oil is it can only get worse, so eventually (before this car leads you into bankruptcy) that will have to be fixed." Bit by bit, I told them everything about the car, just a drip at a time, no reason to sweep them away with a flash flood of less than desirable revelations. Yes, my irascible conscience even required me to report, "You may experience some discomfort of an electrical nature when using the wipers."

You probably think that after all of these endearing experiences with my red '68 Camaro convertible that I would have decided to never own one again. Right? Exactly. Having learned from these errors, I went out and purchased a blue one. In fact, for a short while, I owned both cars simultaneously, thereby falling further into debt than many Third World nations.

My blue Camaro lacked many of the personality traits embodied in the red one. That is most likely because the blue Camaro wasn't a true, 100% thoroughbred, dyed-in-the-wool Camaro. It probably didn't even clear the 50% mark. That's because most of my blue Camaro was composed of after-market body putty. Naturally, the previous owner failed to mention this minor point, along with its faulty speedometer (25 mph slow), odometer (probably about 200,000 miles low), carburetor (how a car could eat so much gas and have so little power would baffle scientists today), and exhaust (with the top closed, the car qualified for the coveted Dr. Kevorkian Assisted Suicide Award for attaining lethal carbon monoxide levels in less than five minutes).

In spite of all its mechanical and structural faults, the blue Camaro cannot be credited with convincing me of the futility of owning a used car. Before I would learn that lesson, it was necessary to purchase five more used vehicles, hitchhike many miles from their broken-down hulks, and spend large portions of my children's inheritance on repairs. No, the blue Camaro's raison d'etre was to teach me about insurance.

Within a year and $1,000 of becoming laden with the blue Camaro, I was awarded two diminutive gold bars, one for each shoulder, and sent on furlough from the federal penitentiary in Colorado. In another year, I would make my way to Louisiana. Once settled into life in Louisiana, a dangerous and frightening situation developed: I was given time to think.

Free time was a new experience for me. I used much of this new found luxury to analyze many aspects of my life. Looking at my insurance bill, I concluded that I could save possibly $200 a year if I dropped every bit of insurance not required by law. Why not? It had been over three years since I became intimate with that guardrail while driving my red Camaro. Why bother with theft insurance? My cars had never been vandalized, unless you count my buddy's girlfriend, who, thinking of convertibles as convenient ashtrays, put out her cigarette on my brand spanking new white top, not that I have a long memory about such indiscretions.

Reaching a decision using precise mathematical deductions and knowledge gained from years of education in the engineer sciences at the U.S. Air Force Academy, I promptly eliminated all coverage, except for the required liability, on both of my cars. That day, my father came to visit. The following morning I took him out to my car to show him the awesome stereo I had recently installed. We were greeted by several gaping holes where the components used to reside.

The next day I walked out to my car to run a few errands. As I approached the car, I saw that my Camaro was now outfitted with a newly installed sunroof! The only problem was that convertibles don't need sunroofs, a fact the vandal who had ripped the top from end to end never even considered. I became more determined than ever to leave my insurance at the minimums. After all, I had to make up for all the money I had just lost to those two nighttime entrepreneurial ventures.

On my way to work that day, as guided by the standards of defensive driving I learned in Mrs. Devers' 10th grade driver's ed class, I decided to pass a turning car by driving around it on the shoulder. My opponent, I mean, the other driver, must have driven 18-wheelers in a past life, because for SOME indecipherable reason unbeknownst to me, he decided to swerve out onto the *right* shoulder in order to make his *left* turn. Thus endeth the saga of my Camaros. The blue Camaro sustained far too much damage to its front end for me to dedicate precious financial resources to its restoration. In other words, the $2.97 I saved in insurance premiums that week couldn't cover the entire cost of repairs. I put the car up for sale.

A couple of weeks later, in spite of the whining coming from a buyer who thought I "would come off of the price at least one dollar," I held firm and actually sold that car in its decrepit condition for a profit. After selling the Blue Camaro, I immediately reinstated every part of my insurance coverage, including the one that reads "Should you be abducted by aliens, we will pay….."

In the coming years, I was to purchase several more used cars and would suffer the appropriate consequences. At least I can say I learned my lesson: No more used cars for me. Soon after the sale of my Camaro, I had to laugh when a friend of mine picked me up at the airport in an old mail delivery Jeep. It was spray-painted white, he used a pair of vice grips as the stick shift, and I could see the road passing under my feet through gaping holes in the rusted-out floorboard. "I would never go this far down in the used car market," I thought to myself, but then again, think of all the money I would save. Low insurance, no car payments…..I wonder if he would consider selling?

Don't Look before You Leap

My daughters (Rachel, 11, and Robyn, 9) and I just returned from our trip to Costa Rica. It was an enjoyable vacation, in that we evaded serious injury and death while rafting down whitewater rapids. We also avoided being bucked from horses, eaten by crocodiles, swallowed by pythons, and covered in molten lava. The trip was barely a day old when our car nearly plunged off of a cliff (I have sworn an oath of secrecy as to which one of us was driving when the incident occurred). We had to wait over three hours in a heavy downpour before a tractor arrived to pull the car out from its precarious position. An added bonus to the trip was the "canopy tour," where we defied death, yet again, as we dangled from the top of the rainforest. If measured on a scale of risk vs. actual bodily injury, this trip was definitely a successful family vacation.

Hanging at the top of the rainforest was perhaps the most memorable event for me, in that I want to remember not to do it again. Securing us from falling to our deaths was the finest equipment manufactured in 1960 by anonymous Third World countries. Although the equipment was a little rusty, it was reassuring to spot at least some clusters of genuine metal molecules on a few of the pieces that held us suspended in midair.

I found the rainforest tour to be the "back to nature" part of our trip. I developed a new found oneness with the environment. Other than putting the recycling bin by the curb every Thursday morning, I never considered myself much of an environmentalist. All that changed as I stood precariously, 150 feet up, at the top of a Ceiba tree. I'll bet that I hugged that tree better than even the most avid member of the Sierra Club could.

After peeling my fingernails from the bark of the tree, our guides gave me the opportunity to zip down a cable to the next tree, and then to the next. I was impressed with the number of straps that they used to secure us before we traversed the forest across that wire. Unfortunately, I also happened to notice that the myriad of straps was connected to just one thing: the rusty, weather-worn pulley responsible for zinging us to the other side. Thanks to my brother Andy, a bungee and ultra-thrill ride park owner, I have experience with these situations.

Before I trusted my life to the workmanship of that pulley and wire, it was time to convert my brain to Scarecrow Mode. Scarecrow Mode is a proven and effective method that is necessary when participating in stupid activities like riding a zip-line between trees or bungee jumping. To enable this innovative style of *not* thinking, it is necessary to pretend you don't have a brain, just like the scarecrow in "The Wizard of Oz." Without a brain, you can't be afraid. Concentrate on blocking out all of the brain's signals, such as the ones screaming "What are you doing up here?" Then, jump.

Unfortunately, sometimes the Scarecrow Mode is overwhelmed by a hyperactive brain, as brains tend to be in times like these. When faced with a hyperactive brain, it may be necessary to enable the brain's rationalization lobe. To enable this latent brain function, you have to fool your brain into believing the situation is harmless. The difficulty is that your brain is smarter than you are. For instance, take the Eiffel Tower in Paris. The Eiffel Tower was constructed in the 1800s for a World's Fair, which means it was supposed to be dismantled about two weeks later. I think the French still plan to dismantle the Eiffel Tower. They just can't decide which union should be responsible for the task, and all of them have been on strike since completing it. As you can imagine, a building that was meant to come down over a century ago makes for a pretty rickety structure today. Your brain knows this; your job is to trick it.

Finding yourself in an unsafe situation, such as near the top of an ancient structure like the Eiffel Tower, you might try telling your brain this: "The Eiffel Tower hasn't fallen down in over 100 years (or at least the French haven't told us if it has), so why should it collapse now, at this very moment that I'm on it?" "Bad luck, that's why. Besides, you're standing near the edge," comes the response from your brain. Shrug off that unsolicited answer and press on, but slowly step back, away from the edge. It's a well-known fact that any tall structure is more likely to fall over if you stand near its edge.

I'm very effective at deceiving my brain by using my rationalization lobe. So, while in the rainforest, I told my brain that by sliding down the wire, I would achieve the desired result of being closer to terra firma. That was a goal that both my brain and I could agree on. *Wrong.* Amazingly, after each trip down the wire, we always seemed to be at least as high above the ground as we were before we hurled our bodies, like George of the Jungle, toward another tree.

That was my experience with the rainforest. My daughter Rachel's take on it was a bit different—she enjoyed it! In fact, after she shimmied up the rope to the first platform, she was so giddy with excitement that one of the guides finally strapped her to the tree. Also, putting us all at risk, she had been hanging *over* the edge of our platform. Meanwhile, the rest of us were embracing the tree so tightly that our faces, like giant blobs of silly putty, had bark imprints on them with all the intricate details of a fossil.

Rachel didn't even mind when she found herself stuck out in the middle of the wire, suspended between trees. As it turned out, she was just a bit too light to make it all the way to the other side, but she didn't care. As she floated 150 ft. above the ground, Rachel just enjoyed her unobstructed view of the rainforest. This abnormal fearlessness of heights leads me to one conclusion: Rachel is not related to me. Sure, she's my child, she even has my dimple on her chin, but the similarity ends there. Otherwise, you might compare the Pacific Ocean to a backyard Jacuzzi and say they are alike because they both foam and contain water. Rachel is clearly more closely related to—and you don't know how much it hurts to say this—my slightly demented older brother Andy.

As I mentioned earlier, Andy currently owns and operates an ultra-thrill ride amusement park. It's crucial to point out that, as a graduate of Harvard Business School, Andy has no monetary reason for owning this park. Like all graduates of L'Ecole des Snobs, he doesn't have to do any *real* work. His daily activities are dominated by golf, tennis, polo, and tracking the value of the stock options he was given by several Fortune 500 companies upon graduation. Most Americans don't know that all Harvard graduates are given millions of dollars of stock options. I'm here to inform you that it's true. In return, the graduates periodically give valuable advice to their corporate sponsors, advice such as: "Your company's product line is too narrow.

You need to diversify," or (several months later), "Your company is too diverse. You need to divest and consolidate." If the student graduated with "honors," like Andy did, he should be able to keep up this routine until he gets bored and decides to retire, somewhere around the age of 31.

Since Andy (age 38) is still "working," I became suspicious of his motives for operating his amusement park. I have now amassed sufficient evidence to prove that the primary reason he opened such a park was to see how many different ways he could trick me, his only middle brother, into strapping myself onto one of his contraptions.

Like a mass murderer, early in his life, there were signs that Andy was headed down this nefarious and sadistic path. There's no point addressing the numerous times that he imperiled his own life. Nor is there reason to discuss the various amounts of damage he inflicted on this own body in the process. It is when I am dragged into Andy's personal little "funhouse" that it is worth remembering.

Specifically, allow me to focus on the time Andy "set" me up with a female friend of his. "Set up"—could there be a more appropriate choice of words? Now you may ask, "What could a date with a girl have to do with any of this bungee and thrill ride stuff?" My point exactly. Does this not illustrate the treachery with which Andy operates? He knew I would suspect nothing as we drove to Pennsylvania to meet this girl. The drive was several hours long, but in those days I was incarcerated at the federal penitentiary in Colorado, also known by the acronym USAFA. The only thing that could have kept me from a date with a girl was…a date with another girl, and trust me, having two dates on the same day wasn't a remote possibility. I was lucky to have two on the same calendar.

Shortly after we arrived, Susan, my date, announced that we would all be going to the local quarry. What fun is a quarry? Well, this quarry was abandoned and since had been filled with water. It was now just a gigantic swimming hole, or so I was led to believe. Passing through a line of trees, we approached the quarry. It was then that I caught sight of The Rock, a protrusion towering about 70 feet above the surface of the water. My knees began to transform into Jell-O. I perceived immediately what Fate had in store for me: I was going to leap from that rock. Why? Because, and I had no doubt about this, Andy was going to announce his intentions of taking that leap himself, thereby leaving me with no alternative but to jump. I looked on as Andy took a gander at the imposing cliff. I grimaced as, inevitably, he declared in a matter-of-fact fashion: "We'll have to go off of that."

In the meantime, we distracted ourselves with a rope that was suspended high above the water on a cable that stretched across the quarry. The launching point for the rope was about 35 feet up. The ride on the rope looked benign enough. Some of the kids we saw would depart the rope at the apex of their swing and perform a couple of flips before entering the murky water. However, my first jump was a real eye opener. At the base of the swing, the centrifugal force was so potent that it required every bit of my strength to hold onto the rope and not let my body touch the water. Believe me, no one wanted to hit the water at the base of the swing.

Susan didn't quite get the message about the hazards of leaving body parts dangling when swinging on the rope. She smacked the water at the base of the swing and was dragged along by the momentum of the rope. Upon exiting the water, she looked as though she had been the guest of honor at a crab boil. Her front half, from head to toe, glowed beet red as though she had been immersed in scalding water.

As we approached L-hour for the inevitable jump off of The Rock, one of the locals attempted what appeared to be a triple flip from a ledge about two-thirds as high. He didn't quite make it, but a few of his buddies were there to jump in and drag his limp body from the water. These adventures in fun at the quarry were not easing my mind about my chances of surviving, unscathed, from the upcoming leap.

Anticipation has always been the most difficult for me. This time it was gnawing me all the way to the bone. Mercifully, Andy finally declared that it was time to go to The Rock. Bravely, I stepped up and declared, "I'll go first." Don't believe me? How unfamiliar you are with my cravenness. There was no chance that I was going to allow Andy to jump first, and unless I was lucky and he died, leaving me all by myself at the top with my jump still to go. It is wise to get jumps like this over with as quickly as possible.

From my perspective atop of The Rock, the people along the edge of the quarry seemed strangely small. It reminded me of a time some years before in Arizona looking over the edge of the Grand Canyon. Okay, okay, so this wasn't as bad as jumping into the Grand Canyon, but fear does strange things to your imagination.

I started about 20 feet away from the edge, stared straight ahead and walked deliberately off into the void. The drop was long enough that I could feel my body accelerating. Eyewitnesses told me that I appeared to go straight into the water. However, when the impact came, it knocked all the air out of my lungs. I quickly made for the surface. Thrilled, not that I had jumped, but that the ordeal was over, I looked up at Andy preparing to make his leap.

Andy didn't employ my "surprise—you're falling to your death" method to trick his, for lack of a better term, brain. Andy stood out as far on the edge of The Rock as possible and gazed downward for an excruciatingly long period of time. For a moment, I thought—no, I hoped—he might just chicken out. I'd never let him live it down. In my mind, I began to rehearse the jabs and jeers that I would employ to his detriment for years to come, 'til death do us part. My hopes vanished as he departed The Rock. He entered the water a couple of seconds later at a nasty angle.

I received a small consolation from the pain Andy experienced from his awkward entry. Of course, I had to ask him why he had taken such a prodigious amount of time to perform his feat. Was he really thinking about not taking that final step? "I wanted to maximize the fear before I jumped," he said. Not normal, I tell you, not normal at all.

Dumpster Diving for Dollars

It's done. No more leaks, no more smells, no more slime. Yes, it's done. At least for today. Maybe. So, how did I become involved in the first place? Purely by accident. Yes, an accident. Considering how this project has transpired, "accident" is the appropriate word. Of course, most people don't choose to have an accident. This choice was all mine; it figures.

I did have an accomplice. Steve, a fellow pilot, just happened to be catching a ride to work on my flight to Miami. The airplane was full, so Steve rode up in the cockpit of the Boeing 757 in one of our two jumpseats. "I see I have three more recruits," Steve bellowed in a voice appropriate for his imposing size.

"What do you mean?" I responded. Steve pulled out the color brochure he had made of his project. The project was a 2000 Dodge 2500 diesel pickup truck. Through a series of modifications, beautifully illustrated in the brochure, his truck now ran on vegetable oil. More importantly, the truck ran on FREE vegetable oil.

Unfortunately, his brochure failed to have a "scratch and sniff" section that would allow the reader to experience the smells he would be submerged in while collecting, converting, filtering, and transferring this so-called "free" oil. Optimistically, I decided to press forward. After all, running a diesel truck on used vegetable oil served one of the noblest of causes known to man: saving money.

Now, I faced a dilemma: Before I could buy I truck, I needed an excuse for buying a truck. Personally, I didn't see a pressing need for one. There were exactly two drivers in my household, my daughter Rachel and me, and there were exactly two cars, a Honda Pilot and an Audi A6. Why did I need a new vehicle?

A strong argument could be made that Rachel's skillful driving managed to keep the Audi in the repair shop roughly 346 days out of the year, thus requiring the need for a new truck, but she wouldn't be driving this behemoth. As a side note, it was Rachel's responsibility to pay for all damage done to the Audi. After giving up nearly her last cent to a body repair shop one day, she dolefully noted, "I wanted a car for going to work, but all the money I made working for over two years has gone into fixing my car!" Another of life's lessons oozes its way into the teenage mind.

So what excuse could I use to buy a diesel truck? Brian. Of course, Brian would be the perfect excuse. My brother Brian recently told me that he wanted a new truck. His 1996 Ford F-150 just wasn't doing the trick any more. Brian felt that the Ford didn't provide him with enough towing capacity. "I need a truck that can tow," said Brian. How many times had Brian attempted to tow anything in the past ten years? None. However, that was beside the point, what IF Brian decided to tow something some day? Hmmm…Now what was he going to do? He needed a new truck!

As a bonus, Brian had mentioned that his wife, Sharon, didn't like driving his truck because it was a stick shift. That settled it. What we needed was every wife's dream vehicle: an automatic diesel pickup truck.

Armed with a fistful of excuses, I began scouring the Internet and the newspaper for a suitable candidate for my experiment. Then, there it was, a 2001 Dodge 2500 diesel pickup truck. It was perfect: leather seats, automatic, four-wheel drive, and already equipped with an extra gas tank and fuel switch.

The next day Brian and I headed up the interstate to Maryland to check out the prospective veggie-truck. The vehicle was every bit of what we had hoped; all that remained was finalizing a price. Had this gent known what an ordeal I was about to go through with his truck, he might have been inclined to just give it us. However, without such clairvoyance, bargaining was in order. Brian left the wrangling to me; he knew I was a pro.

During my Air Force Academy days, Brian was living in Korea with our parents. While visiting my family on the generous three hour vacations allotted to Academy cadets (think chill factor here: the vacations were three weeks, but they *felt* like only three hours), I found that using an English accent while bargaining usually netted the best price:

> Me: "How much are you asking,
> Madame?"

> Korean vendor: "10 dolla."

> Me: "10 dollars? No, no that is a bit
> much, wouldn't you say? Three

dollars."

Korean vendor: "Three dolla? Three dolla? No buy! No buy!"

Me: "No buy? You are sadly mistaken, my dear lady. WE are the buyers. YOU are the seller. Three dollars!"

Korean vendor: "Okay, okay, three dolla."

Off I would go, having successfully acquired a useless brass tiger at bargain basement prices.

Realizing the English accent technique would not have as profound an effect on this truck's owner, I resorted to a more advanced bargaining method: the Uninformed Moron Technique. When bargaining, there is no better way to attain the lowest price than to genuinely believe that an item is worth substantially less than it really is.

In this case, I had printed out incomplete pricing data on the truck. It wasn't until we had the truck back home before I realized what a great deal we had made. As it was, I was going to burn every penny of that savings plus a good percentage of the national debt converting the truck and running it on "veggie."

Running a diesel on vegetable oil is simple enough on paper. You collect the oil. You filter the oil. You rig the truck so that the oil is heated. After the truck is warm from running on diesel, a switch is flipped. Instead of diesel, the heated oil is injected into the engine. Voila, no more gasoline bills.

A strong argument could be made for leaving this entire project on paper and never having it pass the theoretical stage, but no matter, I was determined to convert that truck!

Recognizing that the grossest part of the project would be collecting the used vegetable oil from restaurant grease dumpsters, we "dived" right in, so to speak. Armed with a hand pump I had acquired at a local tool store, and a 55-gallon barrel acquired from a car wash, we pulled up to the dumpster of choice. The Indian restaurant's proprietor had granted us permission to retrieve all of the oil from her grease dumpster that we wanted.

Some of the owner's workers must have suffered from poor aim, because the area surrounding the dumpster was coated with a morass of old vegetable oil and food particles. It was like human-sized flypaper. The shoes we were wearing would never see the inside of a house again.

Next, we removed the lid from the dumpster.

For those who have never caught the scent of the inside of a grease dumpster at the height of summer, I can report that it's an experience worth missing. Flies even stayed away from this stuff, and we all know what they like. However, losing the functionality of an olfactory nerve wasn't going to deter Brian and me from collecting that liquid gold. This smell wasn't gross; this was the smell of money! We pressed up against the sides of the smarmy dumpster for leverage.

Pumping the oil out of the dumpster with our hand pump was a heck of a workout. I'm surprised Brian hadn't thought of pumping dumpster grease before. Pumping grease could have been part of "our" (meaning "my") exercise routine to go along with some of Brian's other ideas like pushing cars and climbing rope.

As we stood there in the greasy muck, getting splashed by errant blobs of vegetable oil, sweat dripping wherever we weren't covered by slime, a thought passed through my mind. I turned to my brother and said, "I don't know, Brian, I think this veggie oil thing is going to really catch on. Can't you just see Mom out here collecting this stuff?"

After roughly 3,157 cranks on the pump, the storage barrel was finally full. We had our first 50 gallons of "free" oil. Our clothes and shoes were trashed, and we were exhausted and covered in slime, but we had that oil! It was time to focus our (my) efforts on converting the truck.

Converting a truck to run on vegetable oil consists of six stages:

Stage One: Configure the cooling system to heat the oil.

Stage Two: Clean up veggie oil spills.

Stage Three: Configure the electrical system to pump the oil.

Stage Four: Clean up veggie oil spills.

Stage Five: Add a separate veggie fuel system.

Stage Six: Clean up veggie oil spills.

Yes, the three weeks to covert the truck to veggie could have been compressed into roughly 35 minutes except for attempting to clean up spilled vegetable oil. Granted, I will confess that on one, okay, maybe ten, occasions I inadvertently pumped numerous gallons of vegetable oil onto my garage floor or my driveway, but that wasn't the reason the cleanups were so time consuming. The reason is—and I was never warned about this: Used vegetable oil can't be cleaned up!

I don't know what happens to that stuff in the fryer, but once it's out, it has a half-life longer than plutonium. Spilled oil will not wash away. Though assaulted with gallons of detergent and even heavy rainfalls, veggie oil remained affixed to my driveway, garage floor, and any rags or clothes with which it came in contact. Little spills I hadn't noticed took on a sticky glue-like nature, defying any attempts to remove them.

Rerouting the truck's cooling system was my first task to convert the truck. The coolant went from a heated fuel filter at the front of the truck to a massive heat exchanger under the driver's seat, and then to a heated fuel pump back near the 60-gallon veggie tank. When completed, the heating system was truly a modern work of art. Of course, just like most modern art, only the artist can truly appreciate it or understand why it was created in the first place.

Next it was time the electrical system. The electrical system had loomed over me like a black cloud. Wires had to be cut. I hate cutting wires. Somewhere deep down in the primal part of my brain, I always suspect there is a good chance I will cut the wrong ones and never be able to recover the project.

As the crucial moment approached, I had an animated discussion with my retired neighbor, Bob. Bob was convinced that I was doing the right thing. "Just cut those two wires there and you'll be fine," he concluded. However, I couldn't shake a sinking feeling I was having. It was the same feeling I used to get during a math test when I arrived at my answers and finished a test way ahead of everyone else. "Could it be I oversimplified the problem? Am I missing something here?" Invariably the answer to those questions was, "Yes!" The big red marks on my paper after it was graded confirmed my suspicions.

I reached with my wire cutters deep into the bowels of the truck's engine. I could barely reach the targets. *Snip. Snip.* It was done. A little splicing here and there, and the electrical system was ready to be tested. I hooked up the truck's battery. *Whirrrr!* The diesel fuel pump screamed, but I didn't even have the keys in the ignition! I flipped the switch in the truck's cabin. *Whirrr* went the veggie fuel pump. Quickly, I disconnected the battery. What had I done to the truck?! Everything was hot-wired to the battery.

Immediately, I called Steve, my pilot friend in Florida. "What did I do?"

"Key-on logic," boomed Steve. "You have to have the key-on logic." What it really came down to was that I never should have cut those wires in the first place. The new veggie fuel pump came with a wire harness that had a convenient plug-in adapter, so all I was supposed to do was unplug the diesel fuel pump and plug in the veggie pump. I had achieved another classic example of snatching defeat from the jaws of victory.

Now, I was faced with having to reach into one of the most inaccessible areas of the engine and attempt to splice new wires to the two wire nubs I had left behind. Covered in grease and sweat, and after an endless amount of straining to reach the seemingly inaccessible wires, somehow I managed to reconnect them. "Free oil, keep telling yourself, free oil!"

At last, it was time to try the system out. Would the truck run on vegetable oil, or was I about to destroy its turbo-charged Cummins diesel engine? It only took a lap or two around the block to raise the engine to its max operating temperature. If I couldn't hear the drumroll as I reach for the fuel switch, I could certainly feel it. *Click!* *Cough. Sputter.* Then the engine roared back to life. It was running on veggie! As I came to a stop in my driveway, air redolent of a fine Chinese restaurant wafted through the truck's cabin. Rumor was that the exhaust would have the scent of French fries, but this was definitely Chinese. My neighbor, Bob, came over to shake my hand in honor of my success.

Triumphantly, I presented the hybrid to Brian. Where had he been during the entire grimy, sweat-filled process? I kept wondering that same thing myself. Odds were that he was firmly planted on a couch, in an air conditioned room, located a safe distance from any possible manual labor.

The conversion had cost over $2,000; $2,000 will buy a lot of gas. The only way to recoup that cost was to drive the truck as much as possible. The plan was for Brian and me to alternate driving the truck based on whoever had to drive the furthest.

The next few weeks were trouble-free except for cleaning up various veggie spills. Some of the spills came from leaks in a couple of the roughly 2,342 new fittings used to adapt the fuel system to veggie. Other spills were from the filtering system in the garage. The most voluminous spills were directly proportional to my stupidity when attempting to transfer the oil to the truck's tank. These were the spills where the veggie oil was pumped straight onto the garage floor.

Other than a minor heater hose leak that disabled the truck near Brian's office; everything was working quietly and hassle-free, sort of like a bomb, just before it goes off. The truck even managed to transport Rachel and all of her necessary worldly possessions to college at Radford, Virginia.

Then, during the return trip from Radford, a little yellow engine light came on in the dashboard. What kind of name is that for an indicator anyway? Last I checked, the engine wasn't gone. In fact, it was still running just fine. As it turns out, the truck's engine light can come on for about any reason, including a defective cup holder. I decided to ignore it and keep driving the truck. Deep down, a premonition of disaster loomed.

Not too much later, the truck let out a cough and began to lose power. Now here's where refined stupidity, attained only by years of practice, comes into play. I decided to keep driving the truck just like it was. The decision was completely logical. The truck ran perfectly well on veggie, going downhill. For going uphill, I switched to diesel.

This driving strategy worked fine for about two days. On the second day, approaching my house, just as it was switched to diesel, the engine quit. That was the last time the truck would run without a significant withdrawal from my account at Fort Knox and a few weeks at Merv's Auto Repair. It's sufficient to say that major, expensive parts had been destroyed.

"So, that was the end of the veggie project," you are probably thinking. Not a chance. It's new, improved, and back in action. The odds of something going wrong have been reduced at least from one in two to one in three. There's even a three-stage, completely sealed (except when it leaks), filtering contraption located in Brian's garage, and the truck is fitted with a low pressure light designed to head off incidents that might try, once again, to send me into bankruptcy.

When will the veggie conversion finally payoff? A quick check of the accounting ledger reveals that the minor incident which required a trip to Merv's resulted in a breakeven point of maybe three years. Factoring in the time and effort put forth and dealing with the stench and the other unique properties of used vegetable oil pushes that break-even point slightly into next century. May I interest anyone in purchasing a veggie-truck?

Bugs

I've always had a fascination with bugs. It's not that I like them. In fact, I've always despised them with a passion. My hatred has never been passive in nature, either. Ever since I first learned to use a magnifying glass, I've taken an active role in trying to rid the Earth of the six-legged creatures. What does a magnifying glass have to do with insects? If you had the temerity to ask such a question, you must be either:

        1. From a planet outside our solar
            system or

2. A girl

In either case, you would be untrained in the uses of a typical magnifying glass on a bright summer day against ants, beetles, spiders (yes, I know they're not insects, but they're just as creepy), flies, etc…

I experience Vietnam-like flashbacks whenever I get a whiff of burnt insect flesh. The magnifying glass is a 10-year old's most potent weapon against a crawling foe. Actually, the sole of a shoe is a more effective, albeit messy technique for dispatching the enemy, but not nearly as sporting. To be sporting, you must have the hunt. Nothing satisfies and entertains more than the hunt. My usual method was to hover above an unsuspecting target using the magnifying glass to focus the rays of the sun in a spotlight around him. As my victim basked in the warmth of the light, swiftly I moved the magnifying glass, focusing sunlight into a narrow beam of death. The bug was only able to take a step or two before it burst into a smoldering, aromatic bonfire of legs, wings, and antennae, which is a fitting death for so vile a creature.

One of my favorite targets was what my brothers and I referred to as a "stubborn" bug. Whatever the official scientific classification of this bug, its title cannot be as descriptive as the name we devised. Stubborn bugs are little brown beetles with a hard shell. They like to walk on driveways or sidewalks until they realize they're being watched. As soon as the stubborn bug knows you've spotted him, he freezes in place. Stubborn bugs are better at playing possum than a possum is. They will not move, regardless of what you do to them. As I, the Grim Reaper, approached, they would sit there like a two-year old with his eyes closed, saying, "You can't see me. You can't see me." The stubborn bugs managed to keep up this façade until the precise moment of death, and only then did they flail about wildly before passing on to a more suitable place: Hades. A kid couldn't have designed a better bug for the magnifying glass. The stubborn bug would never leave you frustrated by scurrying away into the grass. He would sit there, sniffing the air, probably wondering, "What's cookin'?" as the concentrated rays lazed into his tough hide. Moments later, it would all be over for Mr. Stubborn Bug.

In some ways, I was ahead of my time in the field of bug removal. Once, I concocted a special brew of secret ingredients, morphing common household products into the most potent insecticide ever known to man, one drop of which could kill off an entire ant colony. These potions, unfortunately, are not what one would call "environmentally friendly." However, I did devise another contribution to the field of bug removal that was chemical-free and used only all natural ingredients: I had them eat each other. I dropped ants into spider webs, threw grasshoppers and ants to praying mantises, and deposited all sorts of victims on anthills to be torn apart. Modern day gladiatorial combat, and I was… Nero.

I even attempted to use Mother Nature herself against the insects. Once, while living in Arizona, I spent every daylight hour after school digging in ground that was as hard as granite. I made trenches, connecting together all the ant holes in a vast, open field. These trenches were a technological masterpiece, destined to be named one of the Wonders of the World. All that was left was to wait for the rain to come down and drown my pint-sized foes. As luck would have it, Arizona didn't get much rain. Why hadn't someone told me? I was forced to take matters into my own hands. Attaching several water hoses together was just what was needed to move the drowning process forward at a more acceptable pace.

One of the greatest campaigns against bugdom happened one summer between fifth and sixth grades. A couple of friends and I decided to eradicate every water spider in the creek behind my house in Northern Virginia. The proper name for these bugs is "water strider." We didn't know that at the time and tagged them with the much more sinister "spider" label.

This was to be mass genocide. The weapons at our disposal were the reliable and deadly combination of sticks and stones. Of course, the label "stones" doesn't do justice in describing this implement of war. There was variety in our arsenal of stones, each with its own customized use. A handful of small pebbles served as a grenade or cluster bomb. The grenade delivered a lethal spray of stones capable of hitting multiple targets, or at least ensuring a wound to one at close range. However, if the spider was more than six feet away, our grenade was nearly useless; enter the bazooka.

Bazookas had the longest range, and therefore were the most used. The bazooka could be anywhere from Ping-Pong ball to baseball-sized. These rocks, if thrown properly, could destroy a target from at least five yards. Achieving a direct hit at five yards or more proved to be an extremely difficult task. Even more vexing was trying to hit a target at only two feet. Nothing would frustrate an 11 year-old boy more than to pick up the perfect stone, take aim at a water spider floating aimlessly right in front of him, hurl the projectile, and miss by half an inch. With water spiders, if it's not a direct hit, it's no hit at all. That is, unless you use the…A-bomb.

The A-bomb was my personal favorite. Though, I have to admit, its use required far less skill and accuracy than the bazooka, but the effect was spectacular. To qualify as an A-bomb, the rock was required to be so massive that its operator had to use both hands to raise and launch it. Range suffered, so the victim would have to be no more than five feet away. The beauty of the A-bomb was in the utter destruction it wreaked upon an unsuspecting water spider. Floating in a calm section of deep water, the water spider's life would abruptly end as the A-bomb landed squarely on his head. Water would fly up as high as nine or 10 feet in the air. Often the floor of the creek would become visible from the sheer displacement of the A-bomb as it plummeted toward the bottom with its cadaver in tow. A-bombs in action were wonderful to behold.

An added feature of the A-bomb was that, on the chance its user clumsily missed his target; the fallout was so prodigious that it was likely to send the water spider flying out of the creek and onto dry land. There, out of his natural environment, the water spider would be easy pickings. At this point, it was still considered sporting to use a rock to finish the job. Using a rock allowed the warrior the satisfaction of removing his weapon after impact and gaze upon the indentation left in the mud by the water spider's fractured body.

To us, the rock method was an entertaining way of engaging the water spiders, a big game hunt. However, for maximum body count, we made the switch to large sticks. Sticks gave us the advantage of never having to reload and never running out of ammunition. You could use a stick all day without stopping the quest of ridding the Earth of those nefarious invaders.

The soldiers of "Starship Troopers," a favorite movie of mine in which a few humans defend the Earth against hordes of giant insects, would have been envious of our tenacity in the war against the water spiders. We would plod up and down the creek, hour after hour, herding the spiders from one end to the other. It was barbarous; not recommended for those with weak hearts. In the end, though the body count was monumental, I regret to report that the water spiders endured. Nonetheless, there would be new battles to fight on different days and on different fields, and we, the defenders of human kind, would be ready.

Not all of our enemies roamed the ground or floated on water, some took to the air. For years, I awaited the arrival of killer bees in America. They have, of course, already crossed our border with Mexico. I've had a couple of run-ins with bees, so I'd like a shot at these "killers," just

114

to break the tie, one way or the other. The score, so far: bees - one, my brothers and me - one.

The first major confrontation I experienced with a beehive occurred in Virginia. My older brother, Andy, younger brother, Brian, a couple of friends and I were on a Lewis and Clark expedition in and along the creek that ran behind our house. For once, we weren't out on any special mission of destruction, just minding our own business and enjoying the day. As usual, Andy elected to be different and went barefoot. I watched him gingerly stepping from stone to stone, so as not to harm the delicate undersides of his feet. Back and forth we crossed the creek bed, hopping from rock to rock to keep out of the water. Occasionally, we would happen upon a fallen tree that was suspended above the creek. Balancing on the logs was an alternate method for crossing to the other side. Of course, you always ran the risk of slipping or losing your balance and landing on the jagged floor below. Andy's lack of attire left him especially vulnerable to any errors.

On this particular day, we had hiked maybe a half-mile. Most of the "explorers" were walking in the creek bed, but at the time, Andy was standing about six feet above the ground on one of the tree bridges. Without warning, one of my friends screamed in pain. "I'm not falling for that old trick," I thought. All you had to do was react to another boy's feigned terror and you'd become the joke of the day. I wasn't about to shame myself and be the first to react to his howling in pain. He bellowed that he had been stung. Then, someone else cried out that they had been stung. Next, Andy, high up on his log, slapped at his bare legs; he'd been stung twice. Instantly, there were bees, hundreds it seemed, swarming all around us. Andy leapt, bare feet and all, the six feet down to the rocky bed below and took off running. The rest of us were close at his heels, followed by the swarm of bees. Those bare feet didn't slow Andy down in the least. A few more bees found their mark as we sprinted

115

back to the house, running nearly the fastest half-mile in cross-country racing history.

My parents were witnesses to our advance and opened the sliding glass door of the basement to facilitate our, and the bees', entry into the house. Indeed, several bees tenaciously followed us into our sanctuary. That was their mistake. Now they were on my turf. My dog, Heather, a Shetland sheepdog and fearless defender of the family, snapped at the bees. The ones she failed to nail met their end under a fly swatter or a cloud of Raid. We never could figure why the bees attacked us in the first place. Perhaps they possessed that sixth sense that tells when a threat is near. In that case, they might have been right. Targeting a beehive was, in fact, something we just might do.

There was a time when my brothers and I did make a full frontal assault on a bumblebee hive. The bees had taken up residence in my grandparents' birdhouse in Atlanta, Georgia. This attack was a hazardous undertaking. One brother (hopefully Andy), armed with a can of bug spray, would shoot cover fire for another brother (hopefully Brian), who would rush the beehive and stuff tissue paper through the oval entrance. We performed this perilous procedure multiple times to get the hive sufficiently full of flammable material to suit our purposes. To say the least, the bumblebees didn't care for our efforts.

Many a harrowing moment occurred as the "volunteer" approached the hive to stuff his precious load of Kleenex and newspaper inside. The bees would swarm furiously, and occasionally, some of the beasts would pick out one of us at random and launch a counterattack. The winner of this unsavory lottery would vanish in a cloud of dust and screams. Those left as spectators to the event would see their brother dashing away, arms flailing about. The race between boy and bee could cover quite a distance. Usually, a lap around the block was enough to shake them off, but once, Brian was gone long enough to cause us to wonder if the bees had finally won one.

In any just war, there are always a certain acceptable number of civilian casualties. Victory requires sacrifices to be made. In our holy war against the bees, it was, unfortunately, necessary to offer up our unsuspecting mother. Mom sat in the yard, oblivious to the raging conflict around her. As she was in the middle of catching some rays, Mom failed to notice that my brothers and I were experiencing a temporary military setback. We were rapidly retreating from the premises due to a ferocious bug counterattack. As we vacated the yard, the bees spotted Mom.

Several of the bees decided that Mom must be the one responsible for their troubles and vexations. Can't really blame them for that. I've felt likewise myself on many occasions. The bees launched a full-scale offensive with Mom as the primary target. Though untrained in combat maneuvers, Mom nearly vaulted over my grandparents' staircase banister in an effort to escape from the bees. Her agility must have impressed her assailants, because scraped and bruised though she was, Mom entered the house without a single bee's stinger finding its mark.

Eventually, we made our way back to the yard, and before long, we were ready for the Big Event. The custom interior designing we did to the bumblebees' residence had had little effect on their daily activities. They went about their business as though this day was like any other. Little did they realize the peril that awaited their hive. We approached armed with bug spray, lighter fluid, and matches. One squirt of lighter fluid, and the hive was in a frenzy. We patiently waited for the bees' activity to return to normal. Then, we sprayed them again. After several dousings, we agreed that the hive was properly prepped. I believe I had the honor of striking the match. It took me several wild runs at the hive before I coaxed a match to stay lit long enough to ignite the embodiment our efforts. Flames leaped from all sides of the birdhouse. It was our own Towering Inferno, with real, live actors (the bees) performing just for us. The blaze was so glorious that I became nervous it might spread to the fence and even to the house. The bumblebees stumbled out of the hive like drunks. Some flew away, but most fell straight to the ground. We had triumphed over a deadly foe, and once again, made the world safer for mankind.

However, the bees were to heap a measure of revenge upon us. Luckily, that parting shot was aimed at Andy. The following day, we crossed over into our neighbor's yard to survey the damage from behind the birdhouse. Stupidity reared its familiar head as Andy, against our advice, decided to do the recon mission barefooted. One thing any kid knows is that bees are booby-trapped. They don't even have to be alive to nail you with their stinger. As Andy moved in for a closer look, he placed the tender underside of his foot squarely on one of the fallen warriors. Before that day, I never knew Andy to have such natural leaping ability; about a four-foot vertical leap, I would guess. I'd never seen a foot swell up so large, either. You couldn't see any bones from his ankle on down. His foot looked as though it might explode.

Andy recovered from his wound. The same cannot be said of our vanquished foes. Further inspections of the hive revealed that it was *fini*. We had mastered our fears and the enemy. *Veni. Vidi. Vici.*

HeMen

This was a guy's trip, not just because of the lack of any members of the opposite sex, but also because of what we were planning to do. Out on our own, we were going to be genuine cowboys. Naturally, that meant I had to look, feel...no, I had to *be* the part. So, upon my brother Andy's and my arrival in Jackson Hole, Wyoming, we headed straight to the clothing store.

Yes, I know, I know. What was I doing on a trip with Andy—a trip that he had planned? Recently, I've made it a goal in life to minimize the things I have to write about, because most of the time if I have something to write about, it's because I've done something stupid. What could be more stupid than accompanying Andy on a trip into the wilderness? If I wanted to avoid stupidity, this trip was the last thing I should be doing. However, here I was, so when the rangers recovered our bodies, at least I was going to look like a cowboy.

I came out of the store wearing my first pair of cowboy boots, a hat, and a long outback-style coat that made me look just a little cooler than Clint Eastwood and Crocodile Dundee combined. After seeing pictures from the trip, my daughters expressed a different opinion of my looks, but I think my sister-in-law, Sharon's, comment pretty much summed things up: "You look ready for GQ!"

Two other guys, Dave Boggs and Joe Dody, were arriving a little later in the evening. Not only was I going on this trip with Andy, but increasing the odds for "adventure," Joe would be there, too. While up in Alaska one summer, these two guys made Lloyd and Harry from the movie "Dumb and Dumber" look like Einstein and Edison. I don't want to say that I lacked confidence in Joe's judgment, but the last time I saw him, Joe was leaping from a bungee tower at one a.m., nude. What else could be expected at a bachelor's party for Andy? Who knew how much the addition of Boggs, another of Andy's friends, would detract from our overall odds of survival?

I cannot emphasize enough the testosterone levels generated by our anticipation of this trip. We were going to be trained on how to harness and saddle our horses and "pack" our packhorse. "Manny" and "panyar" were just two of the new words we would learn, making us feel legitimate as we moved into cowboyhood. Then, it would be off on our own manly adventure in grizzly-infested wilderness.

This was so much of a guy's trip that one our members (who must remain anonymous because the statute of limitations for his crime has no expiration, so I'll refer to him as AveDay OggsBay) did the manly thing of forgetting his anniversary. Of course, he had a great excuse. During the anniversary in question, we were at the cabin playing a particularly intense game of cards. Therefore, if you ask me, forgetting a little thing like an anniversary was perfectly understandable. It's also worth mentioning that on OggsBay's anniversary, his wife called to inform him that she was bearing him their first-born child—a son (or as OggsBay put it, "She was mourning the loss of her daughter.""). His wife has told him that he will be allowed to return home sometime after his son gets his braces off.

Another thing that proves beyond a doubt that this was a guys' trip was the primary topic of conversation—breasts—or, more specifically, breast implants. This topic was discussed in intricate detail as to the pros and cons of having wives customized in such a fashion. I think our conclusions were best summed up by graffiti that was written and then altered on our dust-covered minivan. Some stranger had written in large letters on the rear windshield "Utah or Bust!" Andy rearranged that slightly to read "Implants or Bust!" Later, by adding the letters "f" and "s," Joe and I finalized the change to "Implants for Busts!"

Yes, I did mention a minivan. I knew that wouldn't slip by you. The minivan was the first shot across the bow of our guys' trip. What were we HeMen doing in a soccer mom special? We should have been on Harleys, a Humvee, or at least in a full-sized SUV, but a minivan? Fortunately, we wouldn't be bringing our vehicle along when we headed out into the bush.

The next step was to get trained at how to be a cowboy. I thought I had done enough just looking the part, but Andy insisted that we actually learn a few things about horses before we took some out as rentals. Boggs, the only PhD among us, decided that his brainpower could be better put to use by staying back at the cabin and charging it up full capacity. Apparently charging a PhD brain requires that the subject lie prone on a couch for no less than 10 hours, carefully monitoring his heart rate, ensuring it doesn't exceed 60 beats per minute. Activities such as cooking and cleaning are strictly out of the question.

Andy, Joe, and I arrived an hour late for our cowboy training. As it turned out, being late wasn't such a big deal. A "manny" turned out to be what is known to the rest of the world as a "sheet," and a "panyar" is a box. The other piece of equipment we had to deal with was called a "rope." We used the rope to secure the mannies and panyars to the packhorse. Our instructors, Steve and Brian, told us that we were learning in one day what trainees did in five weeks. Steve told us the main thing to remember about tying knots is to "Never pull an end through." What a cinch! Was it possible that there really wasn't much more to this cowboy thing other than looking the part? Heck, I was already there on the look, maybe I should have been back at the cabin with Boggs charging *my* brain up to PhD capacity.

Unfortunately, as our training began to progress, it became obvious that Steve intended for us to do things that actually involved the horses. Everything had been fine with the mannies, panyars, and rope, but now we had to get close to the 1,200-pound animals, sometimes down by their hooves. I wasn't too fond about this part, especially when the instructors started telling us tales about guys, sometimes themselves, getting stepped on or knocked silly by horses that just didn't like what they were up to.

Being a genuine cowboy, I was surprised to find myself not liking any activity where I had to reach underneath a horse. I really didn't care for securing saddles or panyars, but most of all, hobbling the horses was something I preferred to avoid. We had to learn to hobble them; because that is the only way we could let them run loose out on the trail without it being too easy for them to make a beeline back to their stable.

In order to hobble a horse, it is necessary to put your head right down by his knee. Once your noggin is clearly in field goal range for the horse, two leather straps are slipped around his ankles, or whatever that area down by the hooves is called. Gently, stroking and talking to the horse the whole time ("Please don't kick me, please don't kick me..."), you snugly buckle each strap. Once secured in this fashion, if the horse wants to go anywhere, he has to jump around like a kangaroo. I could only imagine what might have been accomplished during my childhood with a set of hobbles and my little brother—just another lost opportunity in life because of growing up in the suburbs.

The bit was another thing that bothered me. Horses have big teeth and plenty of slobber, so I didn't like the idea of placing my hand in their mouths while working in their bits. It looked like Andy and Joe had a handle on that part of cowboying, so I gave it a pass, since I figured I would just learn about bits while we were on the trail or have one of them do it for me.

When we returned from our training, there was Professor Boggs on the couch still in full brain-charging mode. It appeared he might even be making a noble attempt at tenure—all in one shot. The rest of that day and the next were spent preparing for the big trip; of course, there was still plenty of time for a little friendly competition.

The basketball games we played had no time limit. They lasted as long as 40-plus-year old arthritic men playing at an altitude of over 6,000 feet on concrete could stand, which should have been about 3.45 seconds, but, instead, it somehow drifted into over two hours. I'm not trying to denigrate anyone's overall conditioning, but if the wind generated from Joe's inhaling and exhaling could have been harnessed, enough electricity would have been generated to power a small city, like New York.

On the other hand, the far less tiring card games of spades were held in an air of gentlemanly courtesy, similar to that which existed between the Russians and the Germans in World War II. We averaged only 637 accusations of cheating per hand. It would have been much easier and less time consuming if we all could have agreed, upfront, to allow teammates to just look at each other's hands before a game commenced.

At last, the big day arrived. I felt well prepared in that I was certain Andy and Joe were packing everything we would need in case of an emergency. Left on my own, small items like matches, flashlights, clothing, and food might be left behind, but not with Andy and Joe. Decades of camping and other outdoor excursions had allowed them to make almost every sort of miscalculation possible. Having learned from the tried-and-true method of "Do not place hand on stove, stove hot," Andy and Joe would ensure our survival. We might not be quite right upon our return, but we would survive.

When we arrived at the corral, Dennis, the owner of the ranch, had all the horses saddled up and ready to go. That was our first mistake; we should have saddled the horses ourselves. No, I guess we had made plenty of mistakes prior to this one—like planning the trip in the first place—so just chalk up this mistake along with the rest of them. The only cowboy thing we were required to do was to manny the panyars to our packhorse, Blondie. Wow! I really sound like I know what I'm doing when I write that. Unfortunately, Dennis had already figured out that I didn't have a clue.

As soon as we arrived, I moseyed (how's that for cowboy lingo) on over to my horse, Thomas, and decided to adjust his saddle. "This is sure to make an impression," I thought. That it did. Adjusting the saddle required me to tie a knot that is about as difficult as tying a shoe. After watching me flounder around for a few minutes ("This goes under here, no, over this one, no, around this, no…"), Dennis reached in a hand, and about 0.6 seconds later, had my saddle safely secured. It was becoming apparent that my authentic cowboy look didn't impress the locals a bit.

Andy, Joe, and I (alias, Larry, Curly, and Moe) simultaneously tackled the job of tying the panyars to Blondie. Why attempt to look stupid separately when we could get it all done in one shot together? The "hands" began to gather around to watch the spectacle. They weren't disappointed, but it could have been worse. The entire process was sort of a repeat of my saddle scene except with lots of arguing and a larger audience ("No, that rope goes over here, no, it goes under here. Aren't there supposed to be two ropes here?) Personally, my major input to securing the panyars was encouraging Andy with these words at the start of his knot tying attempt: "You've blown it already."

Eventually, we had Blondie properly packed. We were ready to go off into the wild as true outdoorsmen, free from the troubles and stresses of civilized life. Men, and men like no other. Undoubtedly, Dennis shared our confidence and enthusiasm, which is why he sent two guides with us. In front was a 16-year-old girl, and bringing up the rear, as a last defense against any wandering, out of control HeMen, was a 10-year-old boy. I don't want to imply that this setup effectively sucked every last drop of testosterone out of our bodies, but I personally didn't need to shave for about week after we returned.

Boggs, in his first act as a genuine cowboy, shot through the head whatever remained of our air of manly competence by attempting to mount his horse from the right-hand side. I know what Dennis was thinking: "I wonder if I should send my seven-year-old granddaughter along with them, just to be safe?" He probably decided that was unnecessary, since Andy, adding yet another notch to our cowboy aura, had already negotiated a price of 1,500 dollars for any horse that was missing, dead, or unusable upon our return.

All our minor faux pas aside, out on the trail, from a distance, we could almost pass for a group of guys on horseback roughing it just like Lewis and Clark. Andy rode Boots. Boggs was on Applejack. Joe guided Blondie from atop of Socks, and, of course, my noble steed was Tom.

Feeling somewhat invigorated at the moment, I decided to gallop Tom ahead to better position myself to take some pictures. Away we went. Okay, so it wasn't much of a gallop, but the gait was close—close to a trot, that is, until Tom's nose went about one hair ahead of the lead horse. We stopped so fast I thought Tom must have released a drag chute out of his rear end. Thinking that there must be some mistake, I made another run at it. *Wham!* Tom left skid marks with his hooves as we slammed to a halt. Tom was letting it be known that there wasn't going to be any galloping free on the range for me. He liked being around the other horses, and that was that.

Our destination was a trough that was located near the area where we would be camping for the night. There weren't too many notable (that is, embarrassing) events on the way to the trough, except for Boggs attempting to mark the trail every 50 feet or so by dropping some article on the ground. The object of choice was usually his ubiquitous bottle of Diet Coke. Fortunately, our 10-year-old auxiliary guide would faithfully retrieve whatever debris we left in our wake.

After a few more hours of riding through the picturesque landscape, a corner of the battered and rusty water trough eased into view. As I dismounted Tom by the trough, it was a pleasant surprise to find that my backside didn't hurt nearly as much as I had anticipated. The slow pace required when accompanied by a packhorse was to thank for my bruise-free condition.

Since we had ridden for hours in the hot sun, the horses would drink gallons, right? Old proverbs don't become old proverbs for nothing. One or two of the horses may have taken a sip, but that was it. The numbers weren't adding up. There was no question about the amount of water expended by our troop, *if* you know what I mean. Tom alone put the most powerful Super Soaker to shame. However, I was responsible for him, and there was no way I was leaving that trough until Tom drank something.

About this time, our guides, confident they would know where to find our bodies, left for the corral. At last, we were on our own and unsupervised—just four guys and our horses against the elements. The first order of business was to set up camp.

Andy and Joe, followed by Boggs, made their way up the grassy slope in search of a suitable area to pitch our tents and to string a picket line for the horses. Of course, their departure left me alone at the trough with Tom. It wasn't long before I gave up completely on trying to coax him to drink. It was time to ride the quarter mile or so up to the camp—at least I thought that would be a fair idea. Tom had different plans.

First of all, Tom was already out of his element. His element being defined as "having my nose right in the butt of the horse in front of me." Situated in such a manner was the only way Tom could experience true happiness. A horse's butt was Tom's 45-inch flat-screen T.V. with digital surround sound and remote, all rolled into one. Without a horse's butt in sight, Tom was beginning to show signs of agitation.

My authentic cowboy hat, coat, and boots didn't ease his fears in the least. I shouldn't have been surprised at what happened next when I untied his halter and attempted to mount the saddle. Tom parried beautifully. As I tried to grasp the horn of the saddle, Tom would spin in a circle just enough to thwart my efforts. We went through this dance a few times until Tom decided he'd had enough. Suddenly, he shifted gears into full reverse.

I had been in a tug-of-war like this before, with my 20-pound dog, Heather, trying to put her in the car to go to the vet. Tom looked amazingly similar to a determined 1,200-pound Shetland sheepdog backing up with all four legs chopping relentlessly at the ground. For about two-tenths of a second, I refused to give an inch. Then I decided it would be inhumane of me to impose my will on Tom by the use of brute force. I also didn't know if my arms were about to be yanked right out of their sockets. I released the halter. Off Tom galloped, yes, *now* he galloped, up the hill and out of sight.

Far behind, I trudged up the hill, sucking in the thin air and cursing Tom under my breath. This breach in etiquette was certainly a blot on my cowboy-like image. As I approached the clearing in front of the woods where our campsite was located, I saw Tom nonchalantly hanging out with the other horses. When I came a little closer he looked at me as if to say, "What took you so long?" As if he didn't know.

It was already eight p.m. If we hoped to have a chance at setting up camp before dark, we had to split duties and work hard. It was then that Joe informed me that each horse required two hours of grazing. Two hours! We had only two sets of hobbles for five horses. Being the mathematical genius that I am, I concluded that even if everything went as planned, we couldn't turn in until about two a.m. It was about this time that I heard a noise that didn't fit in our surroundings—the sound of a car's engine.

There, about 100 yards from our campsite, was an SUV motoring effortlessly along. This was a tough guys' wilderness trip? We weren't even out of SUV range! At that moment, Joe just couldn't help but point out that we could have rented an SUV, not had to feed or water it, and saved about 500 dollars on the trip.

It was a little late for such philosophizing now. We had to get the horses unsaddled, fed and picketed, set up our tents, fix dinner, and have everything hung up and out of the reach of grizzlies before dark. Naturally, I wanted the privilege of being the first to attempt to hobble the horses and see if they would kick my head into next week, but Andy beat me to it. I was even nice enough to allow him to hobble Tom. Making up for the lack of another hobble, Boggs stood out in the grass with Applejack, allowing her to feed.

Although these horses wouldn't drink, they ate so voraciously it appeared that they must have been on the verge of starvation. Speeding up the grazing process, Joe and I divided our activities between holding Socks and Boots, and in time honored camping tradition, fixing the most grease-laden dinner possible: a meal consisting almost entirely of beef, butter, bacon, and cheese.

We concluded that after eating as much as they had, the horses must have been dying to drink some water, so back down to the trough we went. I was guiding Socks and

Boots, if guiding can be defined as trying to avoid being crushed between two 1,200-pound horses who are going to let nothing get between them and their next mouthful of grass. As they gradually drifted together, their rotund midsections began to pinch me between them. Fighting to gain some space, I slammed my body back and forth against their sides. My flailing had a minimal effect on them, but at least I could breathe. Our efforts were worth it, because once we arrived at the trough the horses drank all they desired—nothing.

Back at the camp we had to finish setting up by flashlight. Just after midnight, we finally had the camp in order, and all five horses secured to the picket line we had strung between a couple of pine trees.

At last, I could crawl into the tent and stretch out comfortably in the two square feet allotted me in the space between Boggs and Joe. It was a restful night until about one-thirty a.m., when Joe sat up and said, "I think there's something wrong with the horses." Back out into the cold we went. There's something hard about getting out of a warm sleeping bag and into cold air, and it *was* cold; in fact, there had been a blizzard that very week on the second day of Idaho's so-called "summer."

Wrapped up like some sort of bug in its larval stage, Boggs elected to stay behind and keep the tent warm for us. His plan must have been to release as much heat into the surrounding area as the pinhole-sized opening in his cocoon-like sleeping bag would allow.

I was careful to bring bear spray repellent with me as we left the tent. This was just a precaution. My younger brother, Brian, who somehow managed to avoid this trip, is a bear spray fanatic. He doesn't believe in leaving the bathroom without at least a hand-held model aimed and ready to fire, and that's in his own home in Northern Virginia. I don't want to imply he's a little paranoid, but every time we hear of some heinous crime, like someone snatching a neighbor's newspaper, his response concerning the victim is always, "You know what he should have had? Bear spray."

So there I was, having been trained by Brian, with bear spray at my side just in case there was a grizzly stalking our horses. As it was, we did have an animal problem, but the problem was Blondie. Apparently, she decided she didn't like Boots, who was tethered next to her, so she was kicking the living daylights out of him. We tightened the picket line, rearranged the horses, and went back to a blissful night's slept—until four a.m.

Joe was up again. Personally, after the day we'd had, I could have slept through a stampede, but not Joe. He had no faith in the trees we chose for the picket line. He confessed that he couldn't stop dreaming about the trees collapsing and finding our horses tied up and piled together in the morning, all dead.

It was about then that I realized why the cowboys who trained us kept insisting that we purchase an electric fence to hold the horses. It could have served a dual purpose. First, we would have had a good night's rest, since the horses could have roamed relatively freely within its confines. Also, if it were necessary to get up to tend to some emergency, we could have used it as a cattle prod to get Boggs out of his sleeping bag. Although, from the way he looked in that impenetrable shell, I don't know if the Hoover Dam could have produced enough electricity to rouse him into action.

It was Blondie. She was at it again; this time, Applejack was her victim. Blondie had made several impressions on Applejack's hide and had bloodied up her nose and mouth. We decided to hobble two of the horses and keep all of them away from Blondie. Wouldn't you know it, try as I might; Andy beat me to putting on the hobbles again. He has all the fun. I held the light for him so I could critique his technique (which, in my opinion, was fairly shoddy by cowboy standards).

After what seemed like at least another 30 minutes of sleep, it was time for *most* of us (*if* you know what I mean) to get up and go through everything with the horses yet again. That's about the time that Joe confirmed exactly what I was feeling: "We're not cowboys. It's more like we're babysitters," he lamented. Look at it...sleepless nights, substitute hobbles and halters for strollers, saddles and bits for diapers, feeding time was, well, feeding time, and as Blondie proved, these horses could have temper-tantrums and keep you up most of night. I think we HeMen had been had, and the horses weren't finished with us yet.

That morning the horses weren't too troublesome as we secured their saddles, but something didn't seem quite right. They appeared a bit edgy. It was about then I realized that it might have been years since these horses spent a night away from their corral. Dennis never did pack trips. He didn't mind renting us the horses, but he never did anything other than trail rides himself.

Here were these horses in an unknown location, kept overnight, and led by clueless strangers. No wonder they were starting to go schizo on us. We got a hint that the trip back to the corral might vary slightly from our trip out when Andy started having trouble with Boots. Since I am a cowboy by nature, slipping the bit into Tom's mouth proved to be the simplest task. However, Andy just isn't a born cowboy. I am not the only one who noticed his deficiencies—Boots sized up the situation and refused to take his bit from a no-good dude like Andy. Andy's persistent efforts to force the bit into Boots' mouth finally paid off—at least in duplicating the Lone Ranger's "Hi-Ho Silver" rear back maneuver from Boots.

About that time—although we were deep in uncharted wilderness—Andy decided that the corral really wasn't that far away. In fact, he concluded that he could do the entire trip on foot. However, before we could start our way home, we had to pack Blondie.

We may have looked silly trying to manny the panyars to Blondie at the corral, but now the process became downright dangerous. Blondie probably didn't get a wink of sleep the night before. How could she? She was too busy making sure we didn't get any either. Now, she was becoming a bit agitated with the whole process, or maybe it was just with Andy, Joe, and me.

You know those scenes in Westerns where the horse that is packed full of dynamite starts bucking wildly and kicking up its hooves? Blondie began her best imitation of that maneuver, and it didn't take much to set her off either. The snap of a twig was enough to send her into wild gyrations in an attempt to dislodge all of our gear. The movie industry could use guys like us. They wouldn't even need to train the horses. As a bonus, we could throw in Boggs for comic relief as the heckler commenting safely from the sidelines.

Personally, the idea of transferring the entire load from Blondie over to Andy was beginning to appeal to me. Why not? Andy was already going on foot, and at that point, tying the panyars to Andy would have been a far easier task than tying them to a bucking Blondie.

Finally, we secured the load to Blondie. Three cowboys were on horseback, my brother—the charlatan—on foot. We were ready for the trip back. At last, we hit the trail. Boggs and Andy took a shortcut through the brush, while Joe and I made one last attempt at coaxing our horses to drink. If I had eaten two acres of grass, I'd be thirsty. Who wouldn't? Tom, that's who. You'd think I was trying to feed him cottage cheese laced with caraway seeds and beets. He refused to go near the trough.

Another problem arose as Joe and I caught up to Andy and Boggs; it appeared to me that they were heading in the wrong direction. Far be it from me to question a seasoned outdoorsman like Andy, but before she left, our guide pointed to a gate that she said we should go through and then follow a trail back down to the corral.

An argument ensued. We faced a vexing choice. Whose advice should we follow? On the one hand, we had Andy equipped with all of his years of outdoor experience and a hand-held Global Positioning System (GPS) that could measure our position accurately within two meters. On the other hand, we had the advice of a 16-year-old girl. A minute later, we had all passed through the gate and had it secured behind us. Our decision was not without its price—every few minutes we were subjected to Andy's Eeyore-style whining with statements like: "According to my GPS, we're going in exactly the opposite direction of the corral," or, "We're just getting further away," which he'd moan with his mouth turned down in a half-frown, and characteristically, shaking his head slightly back and forth,

Honestly, we shouldn't have had to listen to such bellyaching. After all, Andy had given up all rights of cowboyhood by choosing to tromp around on foot. Of course, since he was walking, it's possible he may have been a little more concerned about going any distance in the wrong direction than we weather-beaten, range-wise cowpokes on horseback were, but I think the problem really might have been that he was holding his GPS upside down.

At some point further down the trail, Andy smugly informed us that we were finally traveling the right way—as though we wouldn't have made it without his constant updates. I'd like to say that I was surprised by Andy's timely discovery, but call me old-fashioned for using landmarks. Henry's Lake, where the corral is located, had been visible directly in front of us even before we passed through the gate.

Seeing Boggs adeptly handle both his horse and the riderless Boots together convinced me that he truly had made the transition into the Brotherhood of Cowboys. On the other hand, if there was ever a chance for Andy to redeem himself back into the Brotherhood, it was lost on a road a couple of miles from the corral, when he finagled a ride the rest of the way in a car. The least he could have done was to put one of those brown paper sacks over his head (like sports fans do when their team is zero and 20) so no one at the corral would connect him to us, but instead he walked right up to Dennis like there was nothing unusual about showing up without any of his horses.

Joe, Boggs, and I arrived a few minutes later. We settled up with Dennis and ran into our 16-year-old guide, who confessed that she was surprised to see us. Just what was THAT supposed to mean? One of the hands took Boots, quickly inserted a bit in his mouth, and rode him over to the stable. Since I still held the title as an authentic cowboy, I took the time to pose for a few more "action" shots before we left.

The last day of our cowboy adventure was mostly spent rearranging and cleaning the cabin. Later that evening, we squeezed in one last game of cards, at least until things went nuclear. We also talked about next year's guys' trip. The good news? It wouldn't involve even one horse. The bad news? It would involve Andy and canoes. Although a trip with Andy and canoes can't be anything but a losing proposition, now that I've been officially designated "authentic cowboy," I look forward to adding "genuine Indian brave" to my list of titles.

Getting Rich

So you want to get rich? Lucky for you, you've come to the right place. The following pages are the first installment in a series of articles containing my tightly held secrets to achieving wealth. These secrets are the very ones I used to get to where I am today. You, gentle reader, are about to be exposed to all of the knowledge I have accumulated over the years. You will be spared from making mistakes that will cost you time, money, and inflict agony upon your person. How can I make such a guarantee? Because, I have already made most of these mistakes for you.

So without further ado...Wait a second. Already, I can hear some skeptics out there:

"If these ideas are so good, then why are you still working?"

"Why are you wasting time writing about how to get rich instead of just doing more of the same stuff that got you rich in the first place?"

Excuse me for a moment......

BLAM! BLAM! BLAM!

Now that it is just we true-believing, motivated readers who remain dedicated to success, I will continue with today's lesson.

My road to easy riches began by observing my parents. While I was growing up, it seemed to me that Mom and Dad made money without even trying. They did it all in real estate. Every time the Army informed my dad that it was time to move (these orders were timed perfectly each year, occurring moments after I had finally made new friends), my folks would sell our home for some ungodly profit. Then, we'd move to another location and repeat the process all over again.

My future plans for wealth by 25 really began to gel after I observed my dad and a friend of his purchase an investment home in Northern Virginia. I didn't hear much about that home during the next three years that we were away (two of them spent fighting for my life against the poisonous insects of Arizona), but when we returned to Northern Virginia, I witnessed my dad and his buddy sell the home and split an $80,000 profit. Talk about easy money! Do you have any idea how many candy bars could be bought with $80,000? I promised myself that I was going to get in on this gig as soon as I was on my own. It was obvious that real estate investing was a far better way to riches than delivering newspapers while being chased by large dogs for a $1.19 a day. I had already attempted that newspaper/dog method one year while living in Arizona.

To assist me in beefing up my knowledge of the world of real estate, I read a book that Mom had purchased to inspire her before she entered her new job as a realtor. The book was called "Winning Through Intimidation." The primary lesson of that book seemed to be: ·

"Take no less than three lawyers and a few strategically placed hit men with you to any real estate transaction, because the other guy is going to try to take all of your money. It doesn't matter if that other guy is Mother Theresa, in the end, he's going to try to screw you out of all of your money."

The author also insisted that the book was *not* about real estate, but rather, how to succeed in life and love, at least if you are a member of the mafia.

Although mildly disturbing, "Winning Through Intimidation" left me undeterred in my goal to make millions in real estate. Unfortunately, my plans would have to wait until I was released from my four-year stint at the federal penitentiary in Colorado (the U.S. Air Force Academy) and a year of pilot training in Columbus, Mississippi, but finally, my day of freedom arrived.

The old saying in real estate is "Location, location, location." Fortunately for me, after I graduated from pilot training in 1985, the Air Force, in its infinite wisdom, chose to station me in the heart of the biggest booming real estate market in America, the home of legendary skyscrapers, oceanfront properties, and a wealthy clientele ready to do business—Los Angeles, California. Wait a minute. Things didn't quite work out that way. I did have the CHANCE of being stationed in Los Angeles; the other possibility was Shreveport, Louisiana. It was 50/50. Is revealing which assignment I actually received really necessary?

Shreveport was everything; well, it was everything that Los Angeles was not. I can't recall any skyscrapers. As far as waterfront property, the choice was either the Red River or Cross Lake, which contained a healthy supply of alligators. The clientele around Shreveport was more likely to favor a double-wide than a penthouse. There was no equivalent to Malibu in Shreveport either, not that it mattered on my salary of just over $20,000 per year. I couldn't afford much, but I was determined to start my trek toward that first million in real estate riches.

When I announced my intentions to my parents, who were now both active realtors back in Washington D.C., they immediately suggested that I forgo my plans to buy in Louisiana and buy in the Washington area instead. They even suggested that I allow their management team to handle the property for me. What nonsense! Why would I want to miss the opportunity to work day-to-day with my renters? Why would I deprive myself of the joy of collecting rent, and repairing sinks, faucets, and toilets? My parents were so shortsighted.

Pushing their suggestions aside, I boldly blazed my own trail and made my first purchase. The home I found was a late model three bedroom, two bath single family home with a two-car garage. Illustrating the determination that drove me to succeed in the real estate business, this newly acquired investment home was purchased prior to buying one to live in myself. My renters were to have it better than I was.

At the closing, Flash, the elderly notary handling the transaction, insightfully looked in my direction and said, "Sounds like you got a good deal. Now sell it!" What was he thinking? I was just getting started at building my Real Estate Kingdom. Didn't he understand that if this home appreciated just 20% a year for the next five years and if I had another 20 like it, I could retire wealthy? What did he know?

Like the old saying goes, "You can lead a horse to water, but you can't stop him from jumping off of a cliff." I was headed for the Grand Canyon.

The day I took ownership, the house I purchased was in pristine condition. That day was a day to remember. That rental home would never be the same again. After the series of renters I went through, and the destruction they wrought upon that poor, unsuspecting home, it was surprising to find any walls still intact. However, my renters were not the first to rip some rails off of my real estate to riches express.

Almost as soon as the ink dried on the closing papers, oil went from $30 a barrel to $10 a barrel. It was great to see less than $1 a gallon gas at the station again, but Shreveport sat on an oil-based economy, and the foundation had just cracked. Real estate boomed in D.C. as it tanked in Louisiana.

Soon after I had my first renter in the house, the "For Sale" signs began to appear in the neighborhood. I've never read about any research into the reproductive habits of yard signs, but these guys (and gals) weren't wasting any time. Before my first tenant defaulted on our contract (eventually, all of them would), more than one in every three homes was sporting one of those godforsaken signs. Flash had been proven correct in less than six months.

With the home prices falling far below my purchase price, my only choice appeared to be to "gut it out," at least until the market improved or Hell froze over. "My renters will sustain me until that golden day arrives," I thought. They would sustain me the way a spider sustains a fly.

Beth, my first renter, provided an interesting glimpse into human nature. At first, she appeared to be an acceptable tenant. The rent arrived on time and she seemed to be taking care of the home as well as might be expected. Then, Beth came down with Renter's Disease—financial difficulties.

I explained to her that she had signed a one-year lease, but if I could re-let the property, she could go free and clear. Her response was, "I can't have people coming through my home," and, "I can't just leave on short notice." Since she wouldn't let me show the house to other prospective renters, we agreed that all would remain as it had been according to the lease. Two weeks later, the Beth that "couldn't leave on short notice," said she was moving out the next day.

Beth gave the home a quick dust and mop job and then demanded her deposit. I politely pointed out that she had broken the lease, which stated that the deposit would be forfeited. "I'm losing money as we speak," I informed her. I also pointed out that I had no prospective renters, she had turned down my offer to attempt to find a new renter, and amongst other items, the garbage disposal was mangled, as it looked like she had tried to force a dozen, live chickens down it – bones and all.

Beth saw that I was correct in all points, politely thanked me for being a gracious landlord and left. Wait. I'm sorry. That was my fantasy version of the joys of being a landlord. Actually, Beth and her mother thoroughly cursed me out, something along the lines that Hell was too cold a place for me, and drove off, leaving me with a vacant home in substandard condition and a mortgage to pay.

"Beth, please come back!" I was thinking about six months later, after enduring my next tenant. My future as a landlord would involve demolition, eviction, court, and even murder. The good news is that you will experience none of these things, since you will avoid rental property like you would a 30-ton Brussels sprout.

In summary, the first step in the pursuit of wealth is: Avoid Real Estate Rentals. If the urge ever becomes too great, I suggest "simulation." Go buy a game of Monopoly and play until you are bankrupt (it always happened to me). Then, count all of the money that you lost. Multiply by a hundred. Now, smile. Your opponents will be puzzled, but you will be thinking about how much time, effort, agony, and most importantly, money, you have saved by avoiding the real thing.

If you enjoyed this book, the journey gets better. My next book, "This is NOT a Serious Book!," has top secret information on the airlines that no one else will tell you, like, how to pick a flight that will arrive on time. You will receive even better tips on getting rich, bungee disasters, life as a military pilot, plenty of bugs, dogs, snakes, and, of course, my beloved veggie-truck. As a public service, there is also a chapter containing the Theorems of Homeownership. My brothers, Andy and Brian, contribute in their own unique ways, too. It's a fun ride. I hope you'll take it with me.

Link to my Facebook page: David Wesley Webb, Author to receive notification of when the new book is released and for discount codes. (just press the "Like" button)

All of my books are available at Amazon.com and createspace.com/3499776 as paperbacks. Electronic versions are available at BarnesandNoble.com. and Amazon.com.

Visit my blog: 110moons.blogspot.com

Why is it called 110 Moons? Post your guess. The clue is found in one of my books.

Made in the USA
Charleston, SC
24 November 2012